LOOKING AT THE LITURGY

AIDAN NICHOLS, O.P.

LOOKING AT THE LITURGY

*A Critical View of Its
Contemporary Form*

IGNATIUS PRESS   SAN FRANCISCO

Cover art: Illumination from
a 14th century missal
Cover design by Roxanne Mei Lum

ISBN 0-89870-592-4
Library of Congress catalogue number 96-83645
Printed in the United States of America ⊗

Liturgies are not made, they grow in the devotion of centuries.

—Owen Chadwick, *The Reformation*

CONTENTS

PREFACE

There can hardly be a more important topic than the Liturgy if it really is, as the Fathers of the Second Vatican Council maintained, the source from which the Church's life flows and the summit to which that life is directed. Liturgy, evidently, is too important to be left to liturgists. Not only the official liturgical advisers of the bishops but also all those to whom the celebration of the Liturgy is entrusted—and this must in practice mean first and foremost the presbyterate as well as all those for whom the celebration is carried out, the lay faithful—have a right and a duty to be concerned about what happens to the Liturgy of the Church.

'Liturgy is too important to be left to liturgists.' This dictum could also be interpreted as directing our attention to the help that theologians and historians, anthropologists and sociologists, and students of architecture and the other visual arts, of music, and of language might have to contribute to this topic. And in point of fact, in the course of this study I shall be looking in turn at what, in the first place, *historians* can teach us about the recent reform of the Roman rite; at what, secondly, *anthropologists* can tell us; and, finally, at what, in an *omnium-gatherum* term, we may call "cultural critics" can do to enlighten us on this vital subject.

I am grateful to Father Geoffrey Jarrett, president of the Australian Confraternity of Catholic Clergy, for inviting me to give the lectures on which this book is based (at Melbourne, in August 1995) and to my friend Dr. William Tighe of the University of Allentown, Pennsylvania, for supplying me with relevant materials. I regard this small book as a modest contribution to that debate on the desirability of the "reform of the reform" that Cardinal Joseph Ratzinger has called for in the wake of a widely felt dissatisfaction with the present liturgical life of the Latin ritual church in Catholicism today.

> Blackfriars,
> Cambridge, 1995
> Nativity of the Blessed Virgin Mary

I

A HISTORICAL INQUEST

In this chapter I propose a perspective on the recent liturgical reform and, notably, on the antecedents and character of the "Liturgical Movement" that forms its essential background and inspiration.

All historical research and interpretation bear *some* relation to detective enquiry, but as this is not a detective thriller, I feel no compunction about offering my conclusion at the start. Not enough attention was paid to certain ambiguities in the history of the liturgical movement either by those who brought about the Second Vatican Council's commitment to the "liturgical renewal", in the Constitution *Sacrosanctum concilium,* or by those who subsequently worked to give that commitment concrete form in the revised liturgical books whose publication began with the issue of the reformed Roman Calendar in 1969. As a result, the creation of the new Missal and Liturgy of the Hours, as well as the variety of *ordines* that correspond to the *Pontificale Romanum* (for the use of bishops) and the *Rituale Romanum* (for the use of priests and other ministers), was unfortunately attended by infelicities that to some degree provided the occasion for the liturgical abuses that have been so sorry an aspect of Western Catholicism in the last thirty years.

The question obviously arises: What do I mean by "certain ambiguities" in the history of the liturgical movement, which, had people been more aware of them, might well have been better handled, leaving us today with happier results? Histories of the liturgical movement are not entirely agreed on the date of the movement's inception. Dom Bernard Botte, monk of Mont César (Louvain) and one of the principal authors of the revised Liturgy, in his delightful autobiography *Le Mouvement liturgique: Témoignage et souvenirs,* plumps for the Malines Congress of 1909, when his confrère Dom Lambert Beauduin presented a celebrated paper on the participation of the faithful in Christian worship.[1] Botte's chapter on the subject is entitled, accordingly, "The Birth of the Movement" and boldly begins by claiming unanimity in this view on the part of *all* the movement's historians. Dom Olivier Rousseau,

[1] B. Botte, O.S.B., *Le Mouvement liturgique. Témoignage et souvenirs* (Paris, 1973), 18. See also A. Haquin, *Don Lambert Beauduin et le renouveau liturgique* (Gembloux, 1970).

on the other hand, himself a monk of Beauduin's own foundation at Amay-sur-Meuse (later Chevetogne) had taken a very different view in his *Histoire du mouvement liturgique* published a generation earlier, in 1945. What that view might be emerges clearly from the book's subtitle: "A Historical Sketch from the Beginning of the Nineteenth Century to the Pontificate of Pius X".[2] There is perhaps a touch of patriotic bias at work here. A liturgical historian who, though born at Mons, some miles from the French border, belonged to a biritual community of a necessarily cosmopolitan kind would not be likely to ignore Dom Prosper Guéranger, the internationally known founder of Solesmes and author of the multivolume *Institutions liturgiques* and *Année liturgique.*[3] A counterpart who, as his memoirs make clear, was most decidedly a Walloon and quite self-consciously *not* a Frenchman insists that the movement both began in Belgium and was begun by a Belgian. There is, however, more to it than that. For an author like Botte, to whom practical revision of the external form of the Liturgy was

[2] O. Rousseau, O.S.B., *Histoire du Mouvement liturgique. Esquisse historique depuis le début du XIXe siècle jusqu'au pontificat de Pie X* (Paris, 1945).

[3] For his work, see E. Lanne, O.S.B., "Dom Olivier Rousseau, 1898–1984", *Irénikon* 67, no. 2 (1994): 163–85.

exceedingly important and in whose eyes the deci-
sive epoch of the liturgical movement was, therefore,
what we may call its "political" phase, when it set
out to be a force on the stage of the world Church
from 1945 onward, Beauduin's manifesto of popular
active participation in the liturgical rite totally
overshadowed mere attempts to understand and draw
a spirituality from the existing Liturgy, which was
what the nineteenth century excelled in.

However questionable Botte's decision to date
the liturgical movement from that precise year (1909)
may be, his presentation has proved influential,
and not simply among his conationals. Thus Dom
Burchard Neunheuser, monk of Maria Laach, in a
major retrospective on the postconciliar liturgical
reform published in the 1978 *Archiv für Liturgiewissenschaft*,[4] that crucial journal for such questions,
while admitting that in the nineteenth century there
were sporadic phenomena suggestive of the liturgical movement, opts decisively for 1909 as the true
fons et origo, referring to the Malines Congress as
"das Mechelner Ereignis" (the Malines event), with
the perhaps not altogether unintended implication,
to a reader of theological German, that here we
have something comparable, in liturgical matters,
to the role played in salvation history by the "Christ-

[4] B. Neunheuser, O.S.B., "Die nachkonziliäre Liturgiereform",
Archiv für Liturgiewissenschaft 19 (1978).

event" itself.[5] At Malines, so the suggestion seems to run, all earlier types and foreshadowings were fulfilled, and liturgical salvation was at last thrown open to all succeeding ages.

Earlier German commentators, when touching on the origins of the movement, were less inclined to hand the palm to the Latin races. Thus Dom Damasus Winzen located the beginnings in the first "Liturgical Week" held for laypeople at Neunheuser's own abbey, Maria Laach, in Holy Week 1914.[6] Winzen may have been influenced in this choice of a departure point by the significant fact that the previous year, 1913, had seen the enthronement of Dom Ildefons Herwegen as abbot of that community. Herwegen was a collaborator with, and defender of, the most substantial theologian produced by the

[5] Cf. B. Fischer, "Das *Mechelner Ereignis* vom 23. September 1909. Ein Beitrag zur Geschichte der Liturgischen Bewegung", *Liturgisches Jahrbuch* 9 (1959).

[6] D. Winzen, O.S.B., "Progress and Tradition in Maria Laach Art", *Liturgical Arts* 10 (1941). The same view was taken by W. Birnbaum, *Die katholische Liturgische Bewegung. Darstellung und Kritik* (Gütersloh, 1926). The considerably later (1931–1941) scholarly contribution of the abbey to the liturgical movement through its *Benediktinerakademie* is now described by Fischer in his contribution to E. von Severus, ed., *Ecclesia Lacensis. Beiträge aus Anlass der Wiederbesiedlung der Abtei Maria Laach durch Benediktiner aus Beuron vor 100 Jahren am 25. November 1892 und der Gründung des Klosters durch Pfalzgraf Heinrich II von Laach vor 900 Jahren 1093* (Münster, 1993).

twentieth-century liturgical movement, Dom Odo Casel, although Casel's emphasis on the mysteric character of the Liturgy as a participatory reenactment of the high-priestly Sacrifice of Christ and the apologia he mounted in these terms for the silent recitation of the Canon, the *prex sacerdotalis,* render him in some ways closer, as we shall see, to mid-nineteenth-century Catholic liturgiology than to its late-twentieth-century counterpart.[7]

I am not sure whether Botte and Neunheuser were unaware of, or, as seems more likely, chose simply to ignore, what is by far the best researched and most comprehensive study of the genesis of our subject. Waldemar Trapp's *Vorgeschichte und Ursprung der liturgischen Bewegung,* though (as its author admits in a subtitle) principally concerned with the German-speaking lands, also looks around at what was happening in the rest of Europe as well.[8] This book, published at Regensburg during wartime conditions

[7] A helpful guide to the literature by and about Casel is B. Neunheuser, "Odo Casel in Retrospect and Prospect", *Worship* 50, no. 6 (1976): 489–504.

[8] W. Trapp, *Vorgeschichte und Ursprung der liturgischen Bewegung, vorwiegend in Hinsicht auf das deutsche Sprachgebiet* (Regensburg, 1940; Münster 1979). Without mentioning Trapp's book, Neunheuser remarked in his wide-ranging article "Movimento liturgico", in D. Sartore-A. M. Triacca (ed.) *Nuovo Dizionario di Liturgia* (Cinisello Balsamo 1988), 843–56. "It has become ever more clear and certain that the first impulses and achievements of the

in 1940, was difficult of access to later scholars until its republication by photostatic repropublished as it was at Regensburg during wartime conditions in 1940, was difficult of access to later scholars until its republication by photostatic reproduction at Münster in 1979. It is an extremely illuminating document.

First of all, Trapp's study makes it abundantly clear that the origins of the liturgical movement lie in the eighteenth century Enlightenment. In Germany and Austria above all, but to some extent in north-central Italy and France as well, the Enlightenment had known a specifically Catholic incarnation, though not always of a well-balanced sort. Trapp distinguished between what he calls the "extreme Enlightenment", where a secular *Weltanschauung* imposed its own laws of thinking on ecclesial life, and a "moderate Enlightenment" more acceptable to Christian orthodoxy where Churchmen used, rather than were used by, certain aspects of the spirit of the age for the better setting forth of the Gospel. But he nonetheless found in the two taken

---

programme of liturgical reform already existed — in surprisingly clear-sighted and tenacious fashion — in the age of the Enlightenment." Ibid., 843. Trapp is named in the bibliographical notes (only) of Neunheuser's "Il movimento liturgico: panorama storico e lineamenti teologici", in B. Neunheuser, S. Marsili, M. Angé, R. civil, *Anàmnesis* I. *La Liturgica, momento nella storia della salvezza* (Genoa, 1992), 11–30.

together (and discerning the borderline between them is not always easy) some elements closely approximating to certain constituent features of the liturgical movement as he himself knew it in the Bavaria of the 1930s—and some others that were, rather, what he terms "counterpositions". Those latter elements, which Trapp and other Catholic exponents of the pre-1945 liturgical movement—for example, Romano Guardini—abjured, may be rather more familiar to us in the worldwide Latin ritual church of the 1990s. But both those features of the Enlightenment-period liturgical movement that Trapp defended and those that he spurned will repay reflection.

Before we look, however, at what Trapp regarded as the Enlightenment's legacy to the liturgical movement, it will be well to note his own standpoint. His summaries of what the movement represents are a mixture of description and prescription. They are a combination, in other words, of what as a historian he supposed motivated in point of fact the historical agents and authors he describes and what as a liturgist he considered ought to have moved them. Still, these summaries *do* disclose a mind-set and a perfectly sane one. Only in one respect, to be mentioned shortly, would I criticize his point of departure.

Trapp describes the movement as an attempt to recover the essence and inner meaning of the Liturgy as Christian antiquity would have understood

it. It has, consequently, a twofold task: to encourage
"living" (*lebende*) participation in the Liturgy (notice
his perhaps deliberate avoidance of the word "active"
in this connection) and to call people to live their
Christian lives from out of the Liturgy's own spirit.[9]
Two things, he thought, will always suffer where these
tasks are not promoted effectively: first, the spirituality of the faithful, deprived by aliturgical attitudes of the beauty and richness of the spirituality
of the Church herself supremely expressed as this is
in the Liturgy and, secondly, theology, for the work
of God in Christ, theology's central subject, is continued in the Church's activity as mediatrix of grace,
which she fulfills in the Liturgy in a preeminent way.

The thinking of the authentic liturgical movement,
as Trapp would have it, consists in five *Grundgedanken,* or basic ideas. Merely to list these is to show,
I think, the world of difference that separates the
interwar liturgical renewal and much pastoral liturgical effort today. Trapp's *Grundgedanken* are: first,
the mystery of the mystical body of Christ, which is
how he interprets the idea of *die innige Gemeind-
schaftsverbundenheit,* the "inner solidarity of the
community"; second, an unconditional theocentrism
or God-centeredness; third, the glad awareness of
our redemption; fourth, the objectivity of the Liturgy; and fifth and finally what he terms the Liturgy's

[9] Ibid., 1.

happy union of content and form, or soul and body, which I would understand as a reference to the symbolic appropriateness of the ritual activity that the Liturgy prescribes.

The only point on which, with the benefit of hindsight, we need cavil here lies in an aspect of Trapp's stated aims — namely, the reference to Christian antiquity. For traditional though recourse to the mind and historic practice of the Church Fathers is and should remain, the (to Catholics) key concept of doctrinal development tells us, as Newman realized, that patrology is not always by itself a sufficient guide. If that is true of the articulation of Christian thought, we may well expect it to be true in the articulation of Christian worship. As Karl Barth remarks in the *Church Dogmatics,* what is all-important is not recourse to the Church's chronological origins but recourse to her substantive origin, Jesus Christ,[10] and there may be privileged ways in which not only postbiblical but also postpatristic epochs provide desirable means of access to the origin in this most crucial sense. This perfectly valid point, as made by the great Neo-Orthodox dogmatician, confirms at the level of theological doctrine what we could in any case learn from empirical research when, as recently, we find liturgical scholars drawing attention to what has been called

[10] K. Barth, *Church Dogmatics* 4/1 (Edinburgh, 1956), 705.

the "use and abuse of patristics" by those of their number who want to force the data into a procrustean bed and, notably, to make the liturgical forms of the late pre-Nicene age judge and jury over all the rest.[11]

Setting out from this clear position, then, Trapp studies and evaluates a mass of material illustrative of the Enlightenment's contribution for good or ill. What conclusions can be drawn from his survey?

Although the radical Enlightenment of "Western Europe" — Trapp means, essentially, France, England, and Scotland — never became a mass movement on Germanic soil, it did have its influence, traceable in a flow of ideas through the Rhenish prince-bishoprics to Austria, Bavaria, and the rest of south Germany. There it linked up with the diffusion of north German rationalism from the Prussia of Kant and the Saxony of Christian Wolff. Its keynotes were: a utilitarian or pragmatist philosophical infrastructure for which happiness or usefulness is the key to truth; anthropocentrism; a predominance of ethical values over strictly religious ones; a downplaying of the notion of special revelation in favor wherever possible of religion within the limits of reason; and in aesthetics an ideal of noble simplicity, *edle Einfalt.* I shall discuss later the damage that can be done by

[11] P. Bradshaw, "The Liturgical Use and Abuse of Patristics", in *Liturgy Reshaped,* ed. K. Stevenson (London, 1982), 134–45.

ideas of "noble simplicity", but let us note meanwhile Trapp's judgment that this particular feature of the radical Enlightenment produced a Liturgy "as sober and cold as classicism, because it was carried along by intellect and not by the totality of life".[12] The result of the extrapolation of the wider Enlightenment motifs into the liturgical domain was threefold: a demand for the simplification of the Liturgy, an emphasis on its socially useful or community-building character, and the insistence that through as complete an intelligibility or reasonableness as possible it should edify morally those who worshipped by means of it.

Trapp points out the way in which several eighteenth-century Catholic movements, deviant to a greater or lesser degree, both assisted and were benefited by the creation of this package of policy concerns. Late Jansenism, in pursuing its fifth-century Augustinian ideal over against the contemporary Church of Rome, pushed the active participation of the laity in the Liturgy and the use of the vernacular as badges of *Urchristentum,* signs of a primitive authenticity from which the papal Church with her mediocre standards of Christian discipleship had painfully declined. Gallicanism and Febronianism, more interested in Church structure than in spiri-

[12] Trapp, *Vorgeschichte und Ursprung,* 16.

tuality, emphasized vernacularism as an appropriate manifestation of a national or local church and
the right of particular groups of bishops, or indeed
individual bishops, within the Western patriarchate
to alter the Liturgy as received. Vitus Anton Winter,
a theologian under the influence of *Aufklärung*
thought, called for celebration *versus populum* and
the vernacular administration of the sacraments wherever possible not only in the personal or occasional
offices—Penance, say, or the burial rite—but within
the public Liturgy as well.[13] In 1785 the Austrian
government, then in its Josephinist phase of fussy
ecclesiastical interventionism, sanctioned moves to
"declericalize" the Liturgy by opining, via the Vienna
Chancery, that there was no need for each priest to
celebrate daily. Under the impact of the 1786 Ems
Congress, with its markedly Gallican-Febronian
character, the Habsburg State went on to order the
removal of superfluous altars and images and, in
general, a return to the purity and simplicity of the
primitive Church, a *prise de position* echoed by such
bishops as the archbishop-elector of Trier. Trapp
notes in this connection the strong antidevotionalism
of the liturgical reformers of the Enlightenment,
their hostility to sodalities, processions, pilgrimages,

---

[13] J. M. Sailer, *Rede zum Andenken an V. A. Winter* (Landshut,
1814).

such popular devotions as the Rosary and Benediction, and what they regarded as the excessive veneration of saints. Part of the explanation for such iconoclasm lay in their belief that the stripping away of these mediaeval and Baroque excesses would facilitate reunion with Protestants. The attack on sodalities is particularly striking in the light of recent study by early modern historians that has shown how vital they were in the seventeenth and eighteenth centuries in creating what has been called the "Europe of the devout". They were, in more modern idiom, a "networking" of orthodox Catholics, often gathering sizeable percentages of the male population of cities and possessed of a sophisticated communications system that did much to prepare the ground for the mobilized Catholic laity of the post-Revolutionary period.[14] The radical Catholic Enlightenment, in establishing an antithesis between Liturgy and devotions, failed to realize that devotions constitute a major embodiment of Christian mysticism sustaining the liturgical life and sustained by it.

Trapp is at pains to stress what he regards as the diametrical difference, despite surface points of resemblance, between the Enlightenment liturgists

[14] L. Châtellier, *The Europe of the Devout: The Catholic Reformation and the Formation of a New Society* (Cambridge and Paris, 1989).

and the liturgical movement of his own day. First,
the eighteenth-century movement was distinguished
by rampant didacticism. Franz Oberthur, for instance,
who defined divine worship as a "solemn means of
teaching, nourishing, and promoting religion in
the Christian Church",[15] regarded teaching as the
Liturgy's main goal: hence his rejection of, for
example, the Litany of Loreto as purposeless. Something that teaches no clear lesson but gathers up
ancient images in lyrical exuberance around a devo-
tional focus could hardly be anything other than
useless to such a mind. Trapp also points to the
takeover of Liturgy by moralism. Winter (again)
treated the "religio-moral illumination of the intellect" as the primary aim of the Liturgy, the improve-
ment of the heart coming a good second. Again,
Trapp distances himself from a misconceived or
unilateral ecumenism on the part of these commentators, conceding that at one level their distaste for
Marian prayers, hagiological cultus, devotion to the
Sacred Heart, and the use of images and sacramen-
tals derived from a desire to mitigate the objections
of the Reformed to the Catholic Church.[16] At another level, the campaign against those things was

[15] F. Oberthur, *Idea biblica Ecclesiae,* 2d ed. (Sulzbach, 1828),
1:125. Publication of the first edition began in 1790.

[16] A. Vierbach, *Die liturgischen Anschauungen des V. A. Winter*
(Munich, 1929), 17.

motivated by a deficient doctrine of prayer and contemplation, as when we find Felix Anton Blau in his 1788 treatise on the veneration of images remarking that, while prayer is a man's noblest duty, this is only inasmuch as it serves to make the pursuit of his professional calling on earth "lighter, more agreeable, more blessed".[17]

The Enlightenment liturgists offer to our gaze two further traits that may give us a sinking feeling of *déjà-vu*. First, they put forward the notion that pastors—here meaning parish priests—have the right to modify individual celebrations of the Liturgy if this will better adapt it to its twin role of, on the one hand, clarifying the truths and duties of religion and, on the other, inducing a change in the lives of the worshippers. And secondly, they are somewhat fixated on the fourth century. For Winter, only until the 330s did the Liturgy exhibit purity of concepts, noble simplicity, and a proper ordering of parts.

Trapp, from his own standpoint of approving some features of the practical program of Enlightenment liturgists but abominating the theoretical principles on which their program was constructed, is now faced with something of a quandary. How can one be sure of ushering the former through the front door without finding the other sitting in the

[17] F. A. Blau, *Über die Bilderverehrung* (Mainz, 1788), 12.

parlor? He meets this difficulty by asserting a *Grund-differenz,* a difference in the very essence of the two phenomena of the movement then and the movement now. The Enlightenment program was, unfortunately, subjectively based; that of the twentieth century is, fortunately, objectively grounded. The liturgists of the *Aufklärung,* so Trapp thinks, engaged in a process of *ressourcement* to the early Church only when it suited them: only when, that is, patristic practice happened to coincide with what enlightened people would desiderate anyway, with, above all, the removal of obstacles to the plain religion of Enlightenment man. They sometimes wanted the right thing, but they did so generally for the wrong reason. Thus, for instance, their demand for the active participation of the laity had more to do with democratization than with a mystical view of the eucharistic feast — and indeed they avoided the language both of sacrifice and of priesthood whenever possible. Their plea for the vernacular was intimately linked to nascent nationalism. Their preference for the Liturgy over against personal prayer and popular devotion depended on the fact that the latter were regarded as disreputably nonrational; it had nothing to do with true concern for the mediatorial character of the Church in her public offices or the spiritual-metaphysical relation to Christ as Head of his mystical body. Telltale for Trapp is the *Auf-*

klärung objection to the ritual nature of the Liturgy —
its densely symbolic character — as mere objectivity.
There, he says, we see the Enlightenment liturgists
in their treatment of liturgical reform marginalizing
precisely what we today (that is, in 1940) most prize
about the reform movement of our time. And in this
particular sense, then, the interwar liturgical movement could even be regarded as the exact negation
of its Enlightenment predecessor.

What Trapp has so far shown is that a series of
requests found in the modern liturgical movement
can be made for quite the wrong reasons, that there
is an inbuilt ambiguity or ambivalence about the
common list of desiderata that should make us deal
warily in their regard, a conclusion the more impres-
sive in that Trapp wrote as a self-declared apologist
for the contemporary liturgical movement and sup-
ported many of the *Aufklärung*'s concrete proposals.
He assures his readers that they too can safely cast
their vote for these motions because the spirit in
which they are now being put forward differs *toto
caelo* from that of the eighteenth century.

What we, over half a century after Trapp, may
note in our turn, however, is that the approach to
Liturgy that apparently predominates today is much
more reminiscent of the Enlightenment as he describes it than of the interwar liturgical movement
that he presents as its foil. Anthropocentric, moral-

izing, voluntaristic, didactic, subjectivist—these seem
a better characterization, at least in the Anglo-Saxon
sphere, of liturgical attitudes today than what Trapp
would have us be: theocentric, redemption-conscious,
and aware of *seinsmässige Verbundenheit,* "ontological
bonding", with God through the divine Logos in-
carnate, our great High Priest, found as he is in all
his glorious objectivity in the given cultic pattern of
the community of faith.[18] Had we possessed more
discernment, we should surely, in the 1950s and
1960s, have looked with a sharper eye at the grounds
on which a liturgical-reform package was winning
approval. We could have asked whether those grounds
were more "late eighteenth century" than "early
twentieth century". We would then have considered
more critically the claims to well-foundedness of a
series of reform measures that might so easily be
misascribed to, and so become a tool for, the re-
creation of the imperfect attitudes of the European
Enlightenment.[19] At the least we could have taken

[18] Trapp, *Vorgeschichte und Ursprung,* 66.

[19] There was of course *some* awareness of ambiguous back-
ground, notably of the Jansenism of the liturgically reforming
Abbé Jubé d'Asnières and the demands in this area of the 1786
Synod of Pistoia later condemned by Pope Pius VI. Also relevant
is the open letter of Romano Guardini to the bishop of Mainz,
Ein Wort zur liturgischen Frage (1940), most readily accessible in
French translation in *Maison-Dieu* 3 (1945): 7–24. The important
debate (to which Guardini here contributed) over worrying aspects

steps to prepare for and neutralize any undesirable side effects of these potions.

I call the attitudes of the Enlightenment "imperfect" because Trapp is careful not to treat them as totally valueless, particularly when what he terms the "moderate" Enlightenment authors are under discussion. And indeed even the opponents of the *Aufklärung* men recognized their high moral character and the consoling truth that their practice was milder than their theory, as well as the fact that some of the inherited devotions they inveighed against oftentimes bordered on superstition. Although the monasteries were the object of especial opprobrium for encouraging an externalist and fringe piety, German Benedictinism came subsequently to take, on the whole, a benign view of the Catholic Enlightenment, regarding it as a crucible through which the churches of Germany had to pass. Less concessively: the Enlightenment critics were right to stress the need for better instruction of the people through catechesis and preaching (they had more or less created the discipline of pastoral theology

---

of the Liturgical Movement as catalogued in M. Kassiepe's *Irrwege und Umwege im Frömmigkeitsleben der Gegenwart* (Kevelaer 1939), was inevitably overshadowed by the more pressing issues of the War: see T. Maas-Ewerd, *Die Krise der liturgischen Bewegung in Deutschland und Osterreich. Zu den Auseinandersetzungen um die "liturgische Frage" in den Jahren 1939 bis 1944* (Regensburg, 1981).

for this purpose). They were also justified in stressing the better intellectual formation of priests, though their contribution here was vitiated by a somewhat naïve trust in the potency of biblical philology and history and an antipathy toward Christian Scholasticism in all its forms. Their enemies, moreover, were too often impelled, not by a concern for orthodoxy or ecclesial authenticity, but simply by attachment to the familiar and accustomed, regardless of its merits.

If in these ways sympathetic elements can be located even in the extreme Enlightenment, it is not surprising to find that Trapp has good things to say about the moderate Enlightenment, a movement that in general lived longer than its radical elder brother, right into the predominantly Romantic period of the 1820s and 1830s. The actual demands of the so-called moderate *Aufklärung* liturgists were, Trapp admits, much the same as those of their extreme counterparts. What makes them "moderate" is chiefly the grounds on which they proposed their program. They still put their main emphasis on *Verstand,* comprehension, but not now to the exclusion of other human powers. They were more inclined to see the knowledge of the whole man as supernaturally — indeed, christologically — determined. In other words, their anthropology was more fully Christian because their overall picture of reality was more dogmatically defined. They were essentially *via media* figures, practitioners of the *men . . . de* of Greek syntax, balancing the one hand against the other. Typically, they stressed both Scripture and the lives of the saints. They held that the Liturgy should not be too sober and cold but not too sensuous and ceremonious either. They spoke of the Mass as a sacrifice as well as of the assembly of the faithful. They stressed frequent communion but warned against a sacramental materialism where outer reception of the Eucharist would be regarded as enough.

The attempts of the representatives of the moderate Enlightenment to define this *via media* between the thoroughgoing Enlightenment and inherited Catholic practice obliged them to confront some important theoretical issues. The most significant of these was the question: Is the Liturgy primarily latreutic, concerned with the adoration of God, or is it first and foremost didactic or edificatory, the conscious vehicle of instruction of individuals and the upbuilding of a community? This is an issue to which we ourselves shall return, for the way these aims are interrelated is crucial to the evaluation of liturgical reform. As soon as the latreutic character of the Liturgy, now seen as a vehicle of instruction, is downplayed, the instruction it conveys, or perhaps one should say its *celebrant* conveys in interpolating the rite, ceases to be mystagogic and becomes banal. By the same token, a community sense that does not arise from the ritual celebration of worship but is aimed at in and for itself soon appears evanescent or superficial or both and becomes consequently a source of frustration.

Other questions, too, were raised by the search of the moderate Enlightenment for a middle way. For instance, how are outer participation and inner participation to be evaluated in their relative worth? Georg Ludwig Karl Kopp, in his *Die katholische Kirche,* published at Mainz in 1830, regarded outer worship as not only the proper expression of inner worship but also the means to the latter's animation, an important nuance that in effect recognizes inner worship as the more ultimate of the two dimensions. Another major issue was how to assess the relative roles or respective merits of the vernacular and a sacred language. On the whole, if the case for retaining Latin was poorly argued in strictly liturgical terms (for instance, by means of the claim that otherwise the clergy would cease to study it), the case for the vernacular was also marred by the intrusion of arguments based on naturalism, usually of a quasi-nationalistic kind. Typically, Franz Xavier Schmid, in his *Liturgik der christkatholischen Religion,* which appeared at Passau in 1832–1833, proposed a combination of Latin and German, with Latin for the Ordinary of the Mass, German for the Proper.

Schmid also wanted—prophetically!—the restoration of the Offertory procession, concelebration, communion within Mass except for the sick, the reception of the chalice by those laity who wished it, and a reform of the Breviary to prune away unhistorical elements and improve the choice of patristic readings.

It should not be thought that the liturgical ideals of the Enlightenment were altogether a paper religion. Various German dioceses—Mainz (the ancient primatial see), Constance, Rottenburg—showed at least symbolic sympathy for them by measures supportive of *vernünftige Katholiker,* "rational Catholics". Thus in 1785 the archbishop of Mainz forbad the customs of elevating a wooden image of Christ on the Ascension and releasing a dove at Pentecost; in 1809 the bishop of Constance replaced all books of devotion in use by the confraternities with the book of the Gospels alone; and in 1837 a new Rottenburg *Rituale* required the removal of all robed images of the saints.

As Trapp points out, the moderate Enlightenment—and here it really *is* a precursor of the Second Vatican Council—tried to move in two directions simultaneously: toward Christian antiquity (*ressourcement*) and toward satisfying modern needs (*aggiorniamento*). Its plans, however, were never put into practice sufficiently for the realization to dawn that these two directions may sometimes be contradictory and that, if they are, such is the power of *Zeitgeist* that, almost certainly, it is *ressourcement* that will lose out.

One major reason why the moderate Enlightenment did not achieve more lay in its accelerating supersession by the Romantic revival, which had a very different agenda.[20] In one sense the moderate reformers dug their own grave: by trying to alert the radical Enlightenment to the value and beauty of the already existing Liturgy, they prepared the way for those who would see liturgical renewal as essentially a matter of a fuller, more devout and engaged response to what was there, in the books and rites in vigor, rather than in a creation *ex novo* or at any rate in a resuscitation of primitive forms. The rediscovery at the end of the pre-Romantic period of the inspirational character of the Church year, of the cycles of feast and fast, of the ceremonial surrounding the sacraments as something beautifully attuned to move the human heart so that reverence and contemplation could flood in, all combined with wider shifts in sensibility in European culture to explain a new climate in the Church from the 1830s onward. The age of Romanticism had arrived.

[20] For the transition, so far as Catholicism was concerned, still valuable is W. Maurer, *Aufklärung, Idealismus und Restauration* (Giessen, 1930).

The positive feature of Romanticism for our subject is, then, its sensitivity to the meaning and beauty
of the existing Liturgy, a sensitivity in which some
later liturgical reformers were more than a little
deficient. That said, however, early Romanticism in
its treatment of these matters left a mixed legacy to
the later Church just as, in very different ways, the
Enlightenment had done.[21] If the Enlightenment
insinuated into the stream of consciousness of practical liturgists such ambiguous notions as didacticism,
naturalism, moral community-building, antidevotionalism, and the desirability of simplification for
its own sake, early Romanticism contributed such
baleful notions as piety without dogma, reflecting
the idea that man is a *Gefühlswesen* (what really
matters is how you feel), a subjectivism different in
kind from the Enlightenment's and more voracious,
for anything and everything could be made to serve
the production of the Romantic ego; an approach to
symbolism that was aestheticist rather than genu-
inely ecclesial; and an enthusiasm for cosmic nature
(*Naturschwärmerei*) that would see its final delayed
offspring in the "creation-centered" spirituality of
the 1980s. Yet even early Romanticism, by its turn to
the Middle Ages rather than to antiquity, supplied

[21] A. L. Mayer, "Liturgie, Romantik und Restauration", *Jahrbuch
für Liturgiewissenschaft* 10 (1930): 77–141; idem, *Die Liturgie in der
europaischen Geistesgeschichte* (Darmstadt, 1971).

a deficiency of Enlightenment thinking about the Liturgy—since, as already argued, we cannot consistently allow the development of doctrine, but not that of the liturgical life, to proceed beyond the patristic period. And later Romanticism assisted liturgical life and reflection much more substantially, notably in two ways. In the first place, mature Romanticism helped in matters liturgical by recovering the sense that essential to being Christian and even human is an awareness of dependence on what is eternal and infinite, a new Godwardness over against the anthropocentricity both of the Enlightenment and, in a divergent form, of early Romanticism. And in the second place, later Romanticism contributed a better grasp of the Church as a living community, a community, that is, living owing to the vitality of tradition with its supernatural life-transforming power, *not* by punctual or periodic reconstitution as an ethical community ordered to a naturalistic benevolence through moral exhortation here and now. Thanks not least to political Romanticism, there was a rediscovery, in other words, of the Church that bears the Liturgy and whose life comes to expression in it. When the Liturgy is seen as the manifestation of the Church (in itself a perfectly legitimate move), all depends on what doctrine of the Church is presupposed. The theologians of the Romantic period, by contrast with a number of their late-

twentieth-century successors, presupposed a high
ecclesiology of the *Gesamtkirche,* the "total Church",
total both across space and through time, in whose
unity all human ruptures are healed and all the
authentic desires of the human heart find satisfac-
tion and peace. Recovering the Pauline and patristic view of the Church as Christ's mystical body,
such theologians saw her as the mediatrix of grace
with the Liturgy as the objective medium of her
mediating work.

The liturgical theologians influenced in these
ways by a late Romanticism closely connected with a
revival of ecclesiology were not, by and large, much
exercised by demands for liturgical reform, what I
called at the outset the liturgical movement in its
political aspect. It must be borne in mind that
knowledge—even great knowledge—of liturgical
forms and their history does not necessarily lead to
the demand for liturgical revision, just as large areas
of ignorance of liturgical history do not prevent
people from proposing themselves as prophets of
liturgical reform. The point is unintentionally un-
derlined by a story in Dom Botte's memoirs concerning Msgr. Michel Andrieu, editor of the *Ordines
romani* and the early Pontifical, a scholar whose
work remains crucial for the reconstruction of the
primitive Roman rite.[22] On the eve of the 1952

22 M. Andrieu, *Les "Ordines romani" du Haut Moyen Age,* 5

liturgical conference at the Alsatian shrine center of Mont-Sainte-Odile, when a fleet of taxis arrived at a Strasbourg hotel to convey the participants to the venue of the sessions, they left without him. He had just discovered that the conference's aim was the reformation of the Mass on pastoral grounds! Botte calls his attitude an "allergy" but at the same time generously hails him as "le meilleur historien de la liturgie romaine".[23] Though some theologians, such as Johann Michael Sailer of Landshut, who straddled the divide between a chastened Enlightenment outlook and a Romantic sensibility, continued to press for a modest revision of the Missal and Breviary, with some reduction of the cultus of the saints in both and a greater coherence in the choice of biblical readings, they had learned the lesson of the Catholic Enlightenment's mistakes. As Sailer wrote:

> I know it is incomparably better to breathe the letter and spirit of the existing Liturgy as a disciplined cleric can and should rather than to give the prize to the arbitrary, mutually contradictory improvements of the Liturgy by individuals, which lead finally only to a complete liturgical anarchy and, rather than ameliorate the letter of accidental

---

vols. (Louvain, 1931–1961); idem, *Le Pontifical romain au Moyen Age,* 4 vols. (Rome, 1938–1941).

[23] Botte, *Mouvement liturgique,* 105.

aspects, destroy the essence and spirit of the whole thing.[24]

Typical of the Romantic-influenced liturgical theology of the Catholic Revival is Franz Anton Staudenmaier of Tübingen, who sees the Liturgy in, precisely, holistic terms as a divine means for freeing man from fallen finitude and leading him to transfiguration.[25] It is the organ of a community extending beyond this world, a sensuous-spiritual whole, poetic and lyrical in its expression, living and natural in its development, rather than artificially created, a symbolism for the divine created from the contributions of thousands of anonymous pious lives. His Mainz contemporary Markus Adam Nickel will underscore the point in remarking that the seal of holy tradition is lacking to individual theologians, however learned, who would rewrite the Liturgy as they themselves prefer.[26]

It would not be difficult to show that such attitudes are also characteristic of the work of Dom Guéranger at Solesmes. The case made against

---

[24] J. M. Sailer, *Pastoraltheologie* (Munich, 1788), 2:308.

[25] See especially his *Der Geist des Christentums, dargestellt in den heiligen Zeiten, in den heiligen Handlungen und in der heiligen Kunst* (Mainz, 1839).

[26] M. A. Nickel, *Die heiligen Zeiten und Feste nach ihrer Geschichte und Feier in der katholischen Kirche,* 6 vols. (Mainz, 1835–1838; 2d ed., 1863), 1:x.

Guéranger by pastorally minded liturgists is that, in the changed circumstances of post-ancien-régime Europe, the Europe of ideological de-Christianization and the agrarian and industrial revolutions, he and his followers treated the Liturgy as a mere historical showpiece and hence deprived it of its power to be community-creating, something it can be only if it speaks to people as they are. Here we find ourselves at one of the great divides. Recent research into Guéranger's work has shown that the criticisms of neomediaeval irrelevancy that he attracted in the modern phase of the liturgical movement, above all after 1945, cannot be sustained as they stand. So far from being the result of a hothouse aestheticism or sacristy pietism, Guéranger's entire monastic and liturgical revival was spurred on by awareness of the social problem confronting the Church in early- to mid-nineteenth-century France.

The investigations of R. W. Franklin into Guéranger's background show clearly that Guéranger conceived his work as monastic founder and liturgist precisely as a response to the social and cultural *anomie* and individualism of post-Revolutionary France, not in some kind of "precious" abstraction from the same.[27] The question he faced was: How

[27] R. W. Franklin, "Guéranger and Pastoral Liturgy: A Nineteenth Century Context" *Worship* 50, no. 6 (1976): 146–62, gives the essential results.

is Christian community to be re-created? Franklin speaks of Guéranger's answer as a theory of "social prayer" of which the monastic congregation was to be the living exemplar. In the prayer of the Liturgy — this "mysterious means of communication between heaven and earth" whereby Jesus Christ "composes men into the body of the Church"—the supernatural unity of the many in Christ is established and realized. Here we have the clue to the title of Guéranger's last book, *L'Église ou la société de la louange divine* (The Church, or the society of divine praise).[28] It is by acceptance through faith of our composition into a supernatural unity through a preexisting rite that community is engendered, not by the devising of new or adapted rites that have the creation of community as their immediate end. Like happiness, community is not produced by aiming at it directly; rather, it is a vital, indirect consequence of immersion in other things. (We shall return to this topic in connection with what social anthropologists have to say about our subject.) The extant archives of some fifteen parishes influenced by Solesmes and studied by Franklin witness in his words to the "applicability of Guéranger's liturgical emphasis". The liturgical parish was born, he concludes, sixty years in advance of Beauduin's 1909 speech at the Malines Congress.

---

[28] P. Guéranger, *L'Église ou la société de la louange divine* (Angers, 1875).

Here, in Guéranger's work and its repercussions, the quest for community is tied to mystery. Community is to be found *in* the rites as an emergent property of their disciplined form.

What, then, was added to this checkered inheritance by the specifically modern liturgical movement beginning if not precisely in 1909 then on the eve of the First World War? Its chief positive contributions have been twofold. First, there was the scholarly study of liturgical history represented by, for instance, the series *Liturgische Quellen und Forschungen* (both sources, then, and studies) under the general editorship of, successively, two monks of Maria Laach, Dom Cunibert Mohlberg and Dom Odilo Heiming, or Josef Jungmann's *Missarum Sollemnia*, a *summa* of all that could be said about the history of the Mass.[29] These took farther the researches of late-nineteenth-century scholars among whom the English, and therefore predominantly Anglicans, had been paramount. The second contribution of the twentieth-century movement that was the Second Vatican Council's immediate forebear lies in its continuation of the efforts of early- and mid-nineteenth-century liturgical theologians to popularize (in the best sense) an

[29] J. A. Jungmann, S.J., *Missarum Sollemnia: Eine genetische Erklärung der römischen Messe* (Vienna, 1949). Translated into English in an abbreviated form as *The Mass of the Roman Rite* (London, 1959).

understanding of the spirit and texts of the existing
Liturgy—as in Herwegen's series *Ecclesia orans,* of
which the best known was Romano Guardini's *The
Spirit of the Liturgy.* [30] The more ambiguous contribution of the modern movement becomes apparent,
by contrast, when we consider the emerging proposals for practical reform. Leaving aside the handi-
cap, already mentioned, of the protagonists' uncer-
tain knowledge of the historic discussion and reform
attempts of the two previous centuries, we cannot
fail to notice the largely atypical nature of the pastoral paradigms involved. Pius Parsch, for instance, of
the Augustinian canons of Kloster Neuburg outside
Vienna, formulated his program of practical revision,
including *versus populum* celebration, in the light of
—among other things—the experience of the Germanophone Catholic Student Movement, with its
open-air Masses celebrated during cross-country treks
in search of a non-Hitlerite (evidently!) version of
Kraft durch Freude. And a further impulse was subsequently given by another nontypical manifestation
of Church life, the worker-priest movement, where
a priest in some corner of a factory or a worker's
apartment faced his tiny knot of a congregation
over some convenient table.

[30] R. Guardini, *Vom Geist der Liturgie* (Maria Laach, 1918);
English trans.: *The Spirit of the Liturgy* (New York, 1940).

A second questionable aspect of the modern movement concerns the way attempts were made, not always convincingly, to marshal texts that spoke for preestablished conclusions. Botte cites a good example. Though the great majority of patristic texts that treat of the universal priesthood of the faithful do so in an obviously metaphorical sense, with no reference at all to the offering of the Eucharist, and only a few belong within a sacramental context at all (specifically, that of the postbaptismal anointing with its reference to a general priesthood, which is also, however, a general kingship and a general prophethood), some would-be liturgical reformers—and notably the editors of *Maison-Dieu,* the journal of the Parisian Centre de Pastorale Liturgique and certain directors of Catholic Action—would have none of this. What was needed was not such disappointing conclusions, one remarked, but what would "enthuse youth".[31]

How, then, did the modern liturgical movement achieve in the post–Second World War Church what I have called its "political turn"? Pius XII's 1948 encyclical *Mediator Dei* had given the movement at large a pontifical green light (while warning in amber against certain interpretations of Casel's *Mysterientheologie;* but Casel had never been the house theolo-

---

[31] Botte, *Mouvement liturgique,* 64.

gian of the movement, more's the pity in some respects). At the same time, it was widely felt that the same encouragement could hardly be sensed in the cautious and slow-moving Congregation of Rites. The solution found was to prepare private measures of reform and to advance these by gaining the ear of well-disposed national episcopal hierarchies. The international meetings of liturgists that from 1951 onward began to circularize these reform projects were essentially the brainchildren of the Centre de Pastoral Liturgique and the liturgical institute at Trier. The extraordinary thing about these meetings was that with few exceptions they were held behind closed doors, by invitation only, and that even in the case of the exceptions the sessions to which a wider public had entry were always preceded by what Botte calls a *"réunion des techniciens".* Part of the reason for this coyness was, no doubt, fear of adverse reaction by Rome. The presence of the Jesuit exegete Augustin Bea, who also happened to be the Pope's confessor, at the Assisi congress in 1956 induced, it seems, a general reticence among the experts. Whether that was Bea's intention may be doubted, especially since in *Mediator Dei* Pius XII, who was the first pope to speak of the need for public opinion in the Church, had specifically called for an open discussion of at least one crucial issue, the use of the vernacular.

One must, I think, conclude that the principal reason for the adoption of an *in camera* method was that liturgists considered their subject too technical to be safely entrusted, even in part, to the judgment of nonliturgists. Liturgical reform was decided therefore by "reunions of technicians". Considerable continuity of personnel links these reunions of the 1950s to the composition of the consultative body set up to draft the *schema* on the Liturgy and, after that overall statement of principle that is the Conciliar Constitution on the Liturgy had been passed, to the postconciliar *Consilium* that would apply the general principles by the creation of new texts and rites.

This was, then, a revolution by technicians that acquired a generalized stamp of approval from papacy and episcopate. It was not, arguably, preceded to a desirable degree by a shaking of the proposals through the sieve of public opinion in the Church, a public opinion that in the 1950s and early 1960s was more homogeneous, less affected by secular currents of thought, and less preoccupied with issues that, though interesting and important, are not of central importance for the Gospel tradition: in a word, more Catholic than today. Had that wider public opinion been brought to bear, and more especially if the two sorts of voices I shall be describing in the next two chapters (broadly speaking, social anthropologists and cultural critics) had made themselves heard, then the resultant reform might well have been more satisfactory.

As it was, Church authority gave the professionals what almost amounted to a blank check, enabling them to redesign the Liturgy in just that inorganic way against which such reflective commentators on the Enlightenment experience as Bishop Sailer had warned. The provision liturgists made for yet more "creativity" by agencies ranging from bishops' conferences to individual priests ensured that the bills would continue to accumulate as the credit amassed by the traditional rites was used up. We must now turn to examine how social anthropologists and critics of culture evaluated the debt incurred.

II

THE IMPORTANCE OF RITUAL

Reporting on the world of British scholarship, it is a remarkable fact, which has not been as noticed as it deserves, that both Catholic and Anglican social anthropologists and sociologists have tended to take, from the standpoint of their own disciplines rather than simply from personal preference, a somewhat negative attitude toward the mid-twentieth-century liturgical reform that has had so marked an influence on both communions. They have a tendency to think that in the broader lines of its departures from the traditional Liturgy reform may, in certain of its characteristic emphases, rest on a mistake — not a doctrinal mistake, but a failure in human prudence.

The idiom of the writers I shall be expounding is not easy, so perhaps we might begin relatively gently with a text written by an Anglican sociologist whose remarks are, however, highly pertinent to the Catholic practice of Liturgy in the Western Church today. In *Two Critiques of Spontaneity,* Professor David Martin of the London School of Economics attacked what he called the "popular local heresy" of that "cult of choice" that wherever possible opts against an order of rules and roles in the name of spontaneity.[1] Though this "cult" has some respectable origins — he mentions religious notions of conscience and personal decision, and moral ideas of political liberty and existential authenticity, as well as the Romantic concept of genius and the psychoanalytical ideal of autonomy — the tree that grows from these roots has become stunted and deformed. Basically, one truth, or one collection of truths, has been stressed at the expense of the complementary truths that are their necessary counterpart. The result is a dangerous and destructive imbalance.

Libertarians stressing spontaneity — and Martin makes clear that such figures operate not only in civil society but also in ecclesial society and not least in its worship — ignore the preconditions of freedom in a determinate order of stable rules and defined roles that constitute, in Kantian language, the social a priori of personal identity, the latter's necessary condition. In their anti-institutionalism, extreme personalists are sawing off the branch on which they are sitting. "Institutions", in the various

---

[1] D. Martin, *Two Critiques of Spontaneity* (London, 1973), 1.

senses of that word, are needful if persons with a definite sense of identity are to exist at all. When all is said and done, man, though he may not be as context-bound as an animal, is not as context-free as an angel. It is then the *embedded* character of freedom that is ignored by the partisans of spontaneity, and here we must include liturgical advocates of multiple choice, of endless adaptation and unscripted presidential intervention for the establishment of free rapport with others. For such libertarians, "the noumenal self [Martin means the underlying or essential 'self'] is already full of experiential potency. Traditional modes are mere automatic transfers: everyman must start afresh."[2] In the critique Martin is rejecting, traditional churches (that is, churches with traditional worship) are regarded as diverting the impulse to authenticity into "silted channels of alienated tradition and super-imposed forms". Their "received rituals" and "automatic repetitions" are "frozen icons of freedom, stories from which the dynamism has been drained". What the proponents of spontaneity would substitute for these Martin writes of scathingly as a "total and easy immersion in the All". As he warns, "total immediacy produces total relativity." Where each and every chosen expe-

[2] Ibid., 3.

rience is regarded as equally valuable, each by the
same token may just as well be described as equally
worthless.[3]

Writing as a sociologist, Martin asserts the impera-
tive need to defend discipline, habit, continuity, the
located and familiar, the bounded and particularized,
rules, roles, and relations. A rule, as he puts it,
indicates the "existence of a regularity": something
that enables one to anticipate and so to act. Antici-
pating, acting, knowing where and who you are
turn on the due existence of rules. The stability and
definition of the latter are generative of psychologi-
cal health, just as authority and hierarchy, rightly
exercised, are necessary for the flourishing of that
social health which Scripture calls "justice". Without rules there would be only what Martin terms
"unidimensional determination by peers", the law
of the jungle.[4]

Martin regards the ideas of meaningful relation-
ship and significant personal encounter as wholly
impotent when considered as bases on which to
found the life of groups or even individuals. Why?
Because these concepts are virtually without content.
"One seeks for the personally significant [but] nothing is signified." The ideology of the experiencing
self, in whose name traditional forms, including

[3] Ibid., 4–5.
[4] Ibid., 9.

traditional liturgical rites, are rejected, is "literally self-defeating", for beyond a certain point the emphasis on direct experience diminishes the very possibility of experience at all. How constricting, not least experientially, is a liturgy that insists on expressing the experience, the concrete self-understanding, of the immediate group that enacts it.

The experiential illumination of the Gospel depends, Martin considers, on rote and rite. As he puts it: "What is done by rote and performed in ritual provides the necessary substratum of habit on the basis of which experience becomes possible."[5] And invoking the literary critic George Steiner,[6] he asks what must it mean for a civilization to hear the Gospels repeated time and time again in the central rites of the Church. Not only, then, are repetition and ritual form not to be set over against authentic identity. More than this, they cannot be counterposed to creativity either. As Martin writes: "The shortest way to creativity is habituation to technical means of expression and steady soaking in an historical context."[7] And in a daring comparison with the Incarnation of the divine Word, he concludes: "Those who have accepted the conditions of confinement find they are present at a miracu-

---

[5] Ibid., 12–13.

[6] G. Steiner, *Bluebeard's Castle* (London, 1971).

[7] Martin, *Two Critiques,* 13.

lous birth, limited by time and place, fully human, before which even angels cover their faces."[8]

A fuller account in the shape of a Catholic counterpart to Martin's criticism is Kieran Flanagan's *Sociology and Liturgy,* which marries an Anglo-American sociological tradition to the Germanophone theology of Joseph Ratzinger and Hans Urs von Balthasar.[9] Flanagan, an Irishman who is a lecturer in sociology at the University of Bristol, rejects what he regards as a consensus of practical liturgists who favor the maximizing of active participation so as to confer a democratic quality on rite and would keep liturgical symbols and actions as simple and intelligible as possible. Stressing by contrast the ceremonious, formal, and allegorical qualities of ritual as well as what he terms ritual's "ambiguity", Flanagan describes the pastoral-liturgical consensus in bald terms as "sociologically misconceived". It ignores the question of "how the cultural is domesticated and harnessed in a ritual performance that proclaims a distinctive witness."[10] Emphasizing the functions of ceremony, the opacity of symbols, the complexity of actions, and the qualities of beauty and holiness that give the social form

[8] Ibid., 18.

[9] K. Flanagan, *Sociology and Liturgy: Re-presentations of the Holy* (London, 1991).

[10] Ibid., 8.

of rite a distinctive coloration, Flanagan echoes Martin in deploring

> the rise of consumer-friendly rites and a demand
> for loose and lax "happy clappy" events full of meet
> and greet transactions. These trivialise the social,
> preclude deeper meanings being read into the action,
> and skate along the surface of some very thin ice
> where all attention to danger, awe and reverence is
> bracketed. These are rites of the immediate that
> demand instantaneous theological results.[11]

"Liberal" liturgists are in fact dismantling the entire sacred superstructure that rites exist to serve.

The apparent theological strong point of such pastoral liturgical approaches lies, Flanagan remarks, in the notion of the missionary significance of duly adapted rites. A century and more earlier, Dom Guéranger had also spoken of the evangelical power of the Liturgy, but he had seen this as expressed indirectly in its spiritual beauty. Now, however, it is to be expressed directly in a conscious opening of the Church to the world. Unfortunately, so Flanagan explains, this "delivers Christianity to a school of sociological thought that regards rituals as social constructions shaped to express and to mirror the ideological sensitivities of the age".[12] The result is that the rite comes to be seen as the projection of the

[11] Ibid., 13.
[12] Ibid., 14.

dispositions of the actors involved in the act of
worship rather than as first and foremost the work
of grace, a bestowal of transcendence that (to be
sure) *makes use of* human agents for its enactment
but does not, Pelagius-like, *consist of* such agency. In
favor of traditional ritual, by contrast, is the fact that
the quality of habit (one of Martin's favorite words)
endows liturgical action with "an impunity, an absence of worry about the credibility of what is
represented".

As Flanagan would see things, the Second Vatican Council simply took place too early so far as the
history of sociology is concerned. In a retrospective
view of the revisionist phase of the liturgical movement in the period from the Second World War to
the Council and the subsequent reform, he writes:

> Theology inserted the notion of cultural praxis into
> its approach to liturgy, but failed to secure the socio-
> logical instruments through which this could be
> monitored and understood. The relationship of rite
> to the cultural was far more ambiguous and com-
> plex than had been understood at the time of the
> Council. The question of the significance of the
> social came from within theological efforts to renew
> liturgical form—not from sociology. Only recently
> has a form of sociology emerged that could offer a
> means of understanding liturgical operations in a
> way that is compatible with their theological basis.[13]

[13] Ibid., 10.

The principal schools of sociology "available" when the Council opened were positivist, empiricist, or functionalist. Only in the course of the 1960s and 1970s did the stress of the late-nineteenth-century German philosopher of method Wilhelm Dilthey on the distinctive nature of the cultural sciences (*Geisteswissenschaften*) have its impact on sociology, as sociologists began to realize the need for a sociological *imagination* if they were to grasp the meaning of social forms for those human subjects who live in and with them. At last they started to ask themselves how belief systems, now taken seriously even or especially if they were religious, succeed in having cultural expression. Alas, it was then too late for such sociologists to be of use to the actual liturgical reformers. The postconciliar *Consilium ad exsequendam Constitutionem de Sacra Liturgia* was wound up in 1975 through absorption into the Congregation for Divine Worship, that year coinciding more or less with a real turning point in the anthropology of religion as new schools of thought began to emphasize meaning, not explanation, the nonrational as well as the rational, and ritual's transformative power: all of which led to a new respect for the formal, ceremonious ordering of rite, the very thing that avant-garde liturgists most abhorred and the liturgical reform itself preserved only in severely truncated guise. Yeats' rhetorical question "How but in *custom* and in ceremony are innocence and beauty born?" was suddenly grasped in the academy as it ceased to be understood in the Church. And Flanagan suggests (albeit cautiously) that the consequent mishandling of the modernization of rite accelerated the decline of such traditional churches as his own.

He contrasts the impoverished concepts used to "deliver rite to the cultural"—simplicity, intelligibility, adaptation to "modern man"—with the subtle description of the Liturgy given by the Dominican liturgiologist Irénée-Henri Dalmais in his contribution to Canon Aimé Martimort's four-volume study *The Church at Prayer.*

> Liturgy [wrote Dalmais] belongs in the order of doing (*ergon*) not of knowing (*logos*). Logical thought cannot get far with it; liturgical actions yield their intelligibility in their performance, and this performance takes place at the level of sensible realities, not as exclusively material, but as vehicles of overtones capable of awakening the mind and heart to acceptance of realities belonging to a different order.[14]

The first concept to be rendered questionable by both this definition and the sea change in sociological thinking charted by Flanagan is the notion of

[14] I. H. Dalmais, "The Liturgy as Celebration of the Mystery of Salvation", in *Principles of the Liturgy,* vol. 1 of *The Church at Prayer,* ed. A. G. Martimort (London, 1967), 253.

simplicity as a criterion for sound liturgical practice. To the sociologist, it is by no means self-evident that brief, clear rites have greater transformative potential than complex, abundant, lavish, rich, long rites, furnished with elaborate ceremonial. Noble simplicity of rite has been a theme of liturgical reforms since the Enlightenment, as the previous chapter noted. It had not commended itself, however, purely as an anthropological desideratum. It was also regarded as a hallmark of the primitive Church. Though falling outside the sociologist's provenance, this too is now a matter of question. The decision of the postconciliar reformers to return to a pre-Carolingian Roman tradition as earlier and therefore simpler and so better was predictable given the influence on the tradition of liturgical scholarship of the "comparative liturgy" approach pioneered by the South German historian of liturgy Anton Baumstark. Baumstark's book with that title was both liturgiologically pioneering and enormously successful; it was translated into various languages and enjoyed numerous reprintings. However, the work of F. S. West on Baumstark's *Comparative Liturgy* [15] in its intellectual setting has shown that his comparative method was itself drawn, somewhat

---

[15] A. Baumstark, *Liturgie comparée*, 3d ed. (Chevetogne, 1953); the work's original is French, since it began life as lectures to Bauduin's monks at Amay.

strangely, from the biology of the German *Naturphil-osophen* (like Goethe) as well as from the comparative anatomy of such nineteenth-century natural scientists as Georges Cuvier and Charles Darwin.[16] It assumed as a law, consequently, that liturgical evolution moved from simplicity and brevity to richness and prolixity, even though Baumstark had to admit that one could also see evidence of a contrary movement, a tendency later to abbreviate what earlier had been fuller. As the Anglican liturgiologist Paul Bradshaw, now professor of Liturgy at Notre Dame, Indiana, has pointed out:

> This admission that liturgical development might in fact proceed in either direction robs [Baumstark's] classification of any predictive power. We cannot judge a liturgical phenomenon . . . "late" simply because it exhibits prolixity.[17]

Nor, a fortiori, can we make an adverse value judgment on some liturgical rite, text, or practice because it lacks that dubiously reliable hallmark of primi-

---

[16] F. S. West, "Anton Baumstark's Comparative Liturgy in Its Intellectual Context", doctoral thesis (Notre Dame, Ind. 1988), described in P. Bradshaw, *The Search for the Origins of Christian Worship: Sources and Methods for the Study of Early Liturgy* (London, 1992). See now the author's own summary of his research in F. West, *The Comparative Liturgy of Anton Baumstark* (Nottingham, 1995).

[17] Bradshaw, *Search for the Origins,* 59.

tive authenticity. One member of the postconciliar *Consilium* who found the eagerness to apply the criterion of simplicity quite excessive, the Premonstratensian liturgist and author of a standard study of the sources of the Roman Liturgy Dom Boniface Luykx, signified his displeasure rather strongly by transferring to the Byzantine ritual church where he is now abbot of the Byzantine-Ukrainian monastery of the Transfiguration in northern California.[18]

A second concept that Flanagan would see as treated by Churchmen with a marked degree of sociological *naïveté* is that of *intelligibility* in rite. The notion that the more intelligible the sign, the more effectively it will enter the lives of the faithful is implausible to the sociological imagination. It cannot simply be assumed that people will naturally assent more deeply once they have comprehended. As Flanagan explains, a certain opacity is essential to symbolic action in the sociologists' account, so that to attempt to render symbols wholly transparent is, to their mind, a thoroughly misguided proceeding. "[Symbols] proclaim that which transcends the conditions under which clarity through intervention is possible. They embody that which is

[18] P. Galadza, "Abbot Boniface Luykx as Liturgist and *liturgisatel*", in *Following the Star from the East: Essays in Honour of Archimandrite Boniface Luykx*, ed. A. Chirovsky (Ottawa, Chicago, Lviv, 1992).

unavailable to rational manipulation."[19] And if total vernacularization of liturgical language and the insistence on translation styles that win comprehension at the cost of banality were too frequently the result of the principle of immediate comprehensibility in the realm of the spoken word, an insistence on the complete visibility of every detail of what was happening at the altar (and hence not only the removal of rood screens but also the eventual victory of *versus populum* celebration) was its counterpart in the visual realm. Here, as Flanagan remarks, it was not realized that, sociologically, "veiling", "marking a distance", and "tactful reticence" are necessary to reverence. But such terms as reverence, with its connotations of restraint, deference, and awe, soon became prominent by their absence in liturgical discussion.

A third key concept, *community,* has already been touched on apropos of Guéranger. To Flanagan, the concept of community as such—just like that, without any further qualification—is too vague to bear a specifically Christian meaning. Moreover, it can easily degenerate into the creation of a transiently benevolent atmosphere through (literal or meta-

---

[19] Flanagan, *Sociology and Liturgy,* 52. As Flanagan points out, all this was well understood by Casel.

phorical) "glad-handing" (an eloquent Americanism). What liturgists needed but failed to find was a concept of community defined distinctively as the product of a ritual assembly itself keyed into a mystery exceeding that assembly's limits. As the English priest-sociologist Anthony Archer had pointed out in his study *The Two Catholic Churches,* the preconciliar Liturgy at least imposed a ritual authority on all classes and individuals,[20] thus preventing the emergence of groups who would seize the Liturgy for their own purposes or of figures who would treat it as an opportunity for the display of their communications skills. It is not really clear whether clericalism, defined as the undue prominence, within an ecclesial community, of the sacramentally ordained, is less apparent or more apparent in a liturgical rite where the priest is constantly face to face with the congregation and encouraged to introduce some at least of the Liturgy's salient parts, rather than being absorbed impersonally into a ritual role.

A fourth crucial idea, after simplicity, intelligibility, and community, an idea not so much this time in the Council's Liturgy Constitution or any

[20] A. Archer, *The Two Catholic Churches: A Study in Oppression* (London, 1986), 126–46.

official text as in the commentators who took it
upon themselves to interpret the reformed rite to
the clergy and others, was that of *liturgical agency,* in
other words, the role, increasingly personalized and
sometimes in a pejorative sense theatrical, to be
played by the celebrant of the Liturgy and other
liturgical ministers. Here Flanagan notes that, sociologically, a priest cannot as celebrant present
himself at Mass in the same fashion as that in
which he greets his parishioners afterward. The
liturgical role must conceal or at least detract attention from the person, so as to focus it the more
strongly elsewhere.

> The liturgical actor wishes to cast glory onto God
> in acts of worship that somehow minimise or pre-
> clude these elements of worth falling onto himself.
> Like the self, the social has to be present to enable
> the act to appear, but it has to disappear if the end of
> reverence is to be realised.[21]

To the sociological eye, rites work best when they
are repetitive and formalized, so that the liturgical
actor can practice a certain forgetfulness of self,
"playing into" his role, as Flanagan puts it, "em-
bodying the possibility of its existence". In this he
may need a certain distance, at least at points, from
other worshippers. As Flanagan explains, too unilat-

[21] Flanagan, *Sociology and Liturgy,* 44.

eral an emphasis on proximity is sociologically misplaced. Rites that do not allow a sense of distance deny *to the people,* paradoxically, a means of appropriating the act of worship, crippling them just at the point where they could be taking off Godward by a leap of religious imagination. For liturgical actors, though presented within a social frame, have to convey properties of what lies beyond that frame, a rumor of angels.

But where does this leave the notion of *participation,* which is so key not only to the Enlightenment and Catholic Revival discussions in their different ways but also to that modern movement begun in the years before the Great War as well as, and not least, in the papacy's gradual acceptance of its proposals in the pontificates of the last three "Pian" popes, Pius X, Pius XI, and Pius XII? For Flanagan, active, outward participation is to be evaluated according to "the degree to which it generates inner appropriation, interior assent". An English Benedictine liturgist, Dom Bernard McElligott of Ampleforth, founder of the Society of Saint Gregory, had commented on the philology as early as the year of the introduction of the *Novus Ordo,* 1970.

> By using the word "active" for *actuosa* the Church's intention has been misunderstood, and generally, if perhaps unconsciously, taken to mean bodily activity; whereas what the Church really asks for is full,

sincere, mental activity, expressed externally by the body.[22]

As Cardinal Joseph Ratzinger has emphasized, the term *actuosa participatio* at the Council included silence as well as speaking and singing and hence disqualifies any activist misconstrual of "living participation" (as Trapp had called it).[23] Flanagan's interpretation is, evidently, not unwarranted.

The absence in the postconciliar Liturgy of the atmosphere of intense silence and devotion once so striking to observers raises the question as to whether *actuosa participatio,* assessed in terms of Flanagan's criterion, is more advanced or less advanced than it was before the Council opened. Here of course tricks of memory and nostalgia, as well as wishful thinking based on ecclesiastical partisanship, may deceive us. Not every eucharistic worshipper at a celebration according to the *Missale Pianum* before 1962 was burning with fervor, just as not everyone at a celebration according to the *Missale Paulinum* after 1970 is manifestly bored. But a German sociologist's investigation of a large suburban parish in 1960 provides an example of the relatively objective testing possible. As Flanagan comments,

[22] B. McElligott, "Active Participation", in *A Voice for All Time: Essays on the Liturgy of the Catholic Church since the Second Vatican Council,* ed. C. Francis and M. Lynch (Bristol, 1994), 19.

[23] See his liturgical essays in *The Feast of Faith* (San Francisco, 1986), 72.

Many of his subjects reported that they came to Mass to find a space in which to reestablish their spiritual equilibrium, the calmness of the rite—a re-iterated notion—giving a context in which they could adjust the proportions of an often confused existence.[24]

Nor could one accuse Msgr. J. D. Crichton, the doyen of living liturgists in England, of *insouciance* toward the new rites, yet he has spoken recently of a

loss of reverence which ultimately leads to a loss of the sense of the transcendent God who is the supreme Object of all worship. In a way we are in danger of forgetting what worship is about. It is not just a heartwarming experience for those who like that sort of thing.[25]

Or, as Father Anthony Conlon, a London parish priest, has put it in a paper read to the International Eucharistic Congress at Seville in 1994:

The overemphasis on active participation, which only conceives of worship in terms of the community realising its group dynamic through a bias in favour of "doing things", is a serious hindrance to any understanding of the Mass as essentially a litur-

[24] Flanagan, *Sociology and Liturgy*, 63.
[25] J. D. Crichton, "Worshipping with Awe and Reverence", *Priests and People* 9–12 (1995): 453.

gical setting of an historic action of divine mercy
and sacrifice.[26]

Here then it is not simply a question of failing to
advert properly to the divine transcendence in
general. More devastatingly, when the Mass is at
issue, there is inadequate advertence to that supreme
act whereby the divine transcendence engaged itself
in trinitarian fashion for our definitive salvation on
Calvary, when the Son offered himself to the Father
in the Spirit so that his Sacrifice could be fruitful in
the renewed pouring out of himself in the propitia-
tory intercession of the Eucharist and its foundation
in his High Priestly prayer in the heavens.

> Too much can be centered on the contribution made
> by the participants as though that alone made for
> the efficacy of the Eucharist and less attention — if
> any — may be paid to the sacramental offering of the
> great High Priest.[27]

The fact that in many parish celebrations the
church building is evidently regarded as simply an
assembly point before Mass starts and a place of

[26] A. Conlon, "The Participation of the Faithful in the Post-
Conciliar Liturgy: A Critical Perspective on Contemporary
Practice" in *XLV Conventus Eucharisticus Internationalis, Sevilla
1–13.vi.1993, Christus Lumen Gentium, Eucharistia et Evangelizatio*
(Vatican City, 1993), 573.
[27] Ibid.

concourse when Mass ends, in sharp contrast to the former practice when many people made prayers of preparation before Mass and prayers of thanksgiving after it and certainly were not disabled in so doing by other worshippers, points toward the same conclusion. If active participation is rightly evaluated by the quality of inner participation it arouses, then, it would seem, it has not yet succeeded in its task.

What from the sociologist's standpoint has been overlooked is that, as Flanagan remarks, liturgical forms operate in the manner of icons—opening up a sense of the presence of the divine, not of course by the painterly means of color and line, but through social actions believed to be endowed and intended to be endowed with "holy purpose".

Flanagan's overall conclusion is that the Roman Liturgy has fallen into the hands of "convivial Puritans". For these, procedures for worship are to be kept as simple as possible so as to maximize social relationships in the production of the rite. A ritual minimalism serves to sustain a relaxed atmosphere where all may contribute informally. "Bind us together" is the theme song of a liturgical life where hierarchy and ceremony are treated as deleterious to happy togetherness.

To Flanagan, as to Martin, this is simply wrongheaded. Informal or endlessly adaptable Liturgy may be *beau mais ce n'est pas la guerre.* The shape of the rite takes on "unfruitful unpredictability", impairing its claim to constitute, indeed, a public order of worship. As the phenomenologist of religion Rudolf Otto saw at the beginning of this century, an undisciplined rite clamantly asserting direct links with the production of the numinous has little chance of representing the latter successfully when compared with one that humbly petitions the holy in solemn mode. Such tacit, mysterious qualities of rite, Flanagan continues, are, moreover, what permit its endless replaying. He likens to this the way a literary classic (*The Brothers Karamazov, Moby Dick*) can be endlessly reread if it be in a positive sense "ambiguous", namely, not increasing the reader's uncertainty about meaning but rather maintaining openness to ultimate meaning (the sacred). Repeated use, so Flanagan concludes: "generates a passage of growth into understanding the implications of what cannot be grasped, and at the same time fuels a wish to have more revealed from what is concealed."[28] The message is that the adhesive that holds rites together has become too diluted to stick, and Flanagan looks to older forms of the Latin Liturgy for assistance when he writes: "Formal traditional forms of rite cannot be dismissed as being inherently cultur-

[28] Flanagan, *Sociology and Liturgy,* 308.

ally incredible. These rites only become incredible when they are deemed to be so."[29]

That is also very much the Gospel according to the English Catholic social anthropologists who have devoted thought to our issue: Professor Mary Douglas of London University and the late Professor Victor Turner, who at the end of his professional career crossed the Atlantic to a chair at the University of Chicago.

Mary Douglas opened her study *Natural Symbols: Explorations in Cosmology* with an essay entitled "Away from Ritual", which had appeared in somewhat different form in the house journal of the English Dominicans as "The Contempt of Ritual" in the summer of 1968.[30] She warns that contempt for ritual forms eventually leads people to take a purely private view of religious experience, from where it is only a short step to the frank avowal of humanism.

One feature distinguishing social anthropologists from sociologists is that the former have a much more formidable, not to say sometimes impenetrable, conceptual apparatus at their disposal. The most easily grasped aspect of Douglas' essay is her critique of the abolition by the bishops of England and

[29] Ibid., 325.

[30] M. Douglas, "The Contempt of Ritual", *New Blackfriars* 49, nos. 577–78 (1968): 475–82; 528–39; idem, *Natural Symbols: Explorations in Cosmology* (London, 1970).

Wales of compulsory abstinence from fleshfoods on Fridays, and this contains at any rate some major clues helpful in unravelling her approach. The Friday abstinence is the only ritual that brings Christian symbols into kitchen and larder. Taking away one symbol that means something in that domain is, she pointed out, no guarantee that the spirit of a generalized charity will reign (as the bishops piously hoped) in its stead. It would have been preferable to have built upon this weekly ritual rather than to have sought platitudinous substitutes for it. Her explanation, as an anthropologist, for the bishops' decision to abandon Friday abstinence is not especially flattering. Owing to the manner of their education—she refers to the *embourgeoisement* of those whose families were once working class—the bishops were predictably peculiarly insensitive to nonverbal signals. The decision symptomizes this age of the Church: "It is as if the liturgical signal boxes were manned by colour blind signalmen."[31]

The issue of Friday abstinence raises for her the whole question of the contemporary Church's approach to ritual—to symbolically intense bodily activity as used in the worship of God. Her deeper argument is that the cosmos—the fundamental order of reality, including social reality—is always

[31] Douglas, *Natural Symbols,* 42.

seen through the medium of the body, and notably through the kinds and range of actions in which the body intersects with nature and other people. Appealing to the exploration of family structure made in the 1960s by her secular colleague Basil Bernstein,[32] Douglas proposes that children whose families are "personal" rather than "positional"—children, that is, who come from families where common life and hierarchy are minimized in favor of, at least ideally, a unique communication between parent, on the one hand, and, on the other, each individual child— are likely to grow up with ears unattuned to the unspoken messages of ritual codes. And yet, as there is in fact no human being whose life does *not* need to "unfold in a coherent symbolic system", those who resist ritual are missing out on something essential to humanity as such.

> Such non-verbal symbols are capable of creating a structure of meaning, in which individuals can relate to one another and realise their own ultimate purposes. . . . Alas for the child from the personal home who longs for non-verbal forms of relationship but has only been equipped with words and a contempt for ritual forms. By rejecting ritualised speech he rejects his own faculty for pushing back the boundaries between inside and outside so as to

[32] B. Bernstein, "Social Class and Psychotherapy", *British Journal of Sociology* 15 (1964): 54–64.

incorporate in himself a patterned social world. At the same time, he thwarts his faculty for receiving immediate, condensed messages given obliquely along non-verbal channels.[33]

This statement, incidentally, tells us much about the new phenomenon of Catholic individualism understood as the systematic disparagement of common structure, hierarchical authority, and traditional liturgy alike.

Among the causes of antiritualism, then, Mary Douglas places first and foremost social change. But if social change naturally tends to prompt a new cosmology, a new set of spectacles for looking at the world, then those concerned for the health of Catholic Christianity, which has its own cosmology based on traditional ritual, on the sacraments, and ultimately on the Incarnation, must try to break this causal chain. The slackening of group and grid whereby change in social patterns, especially in the family, brings about contempt for rite, the lack of strong social articulation in an increasingly amorphous, excessively personalized, individualized, and dehierarchicalized world: these processes, left to themselves, will tend to produce a "religion of effervescence", incompatible with a sacramental faith. Writing in the immediate aftermath of the appear-

[33] Douglas, *Natural Symbols,* 53.

ance of a euphoric Western European and North American radicalism in the late 1960s, she comments:

> This is the sector of society which we expect to be weak in its perception of condensed symbols, preferring diffuse, emotive symbols of mass effect. The religious style is spontaneity, enthusiasm and effervescence. Bodily disassociation in trance, induced by dance or drugs, is valued along with other symbols of non-differentiation. Distinguishing social categories are devalued, but the individual is exalted. The self is presented without inhibition or shyness. There is little or no self-consciousness about sexual or other bodily orifices and functions. As to intellectual style, there is little concern with differentiated units of time, respect for past or programme for the future. The dead are forgotten. Intellectual discriminations are not useful or valued.

And she concludes:

> The general tone of this cosmological style is to express the current social experience. In the latter there is minimum differentiation and organisation: symbolic behaviour reflects this lack. In the field of intellect it is disastrous.[34]

Relating all this to the Church, Douglas maintains that antiritualism is of a piece with the "generous warmth" of the "doctrinal latitude" of "reforming bishops and radical theologians", their "critical dis-

[34] Ibid., 149.

solving of categories and attack on intellectual and administrative distinctions".[35] In her view, all these developments are generated by a particular social experience, that of unrestricted personalism, but the cosmology they promote is manifestly deficient from the standpoint both of the life of the mind at large and more especially that of the Christian intelligence. In her own idiom, "The value of particular social forms can only be judged objectively by the analytic power of the elaborated code": in other words, to decode *that* remark (!), the mediocrity of the spiritual and theological life typically produced by an antiritualist Church is the best possible proof of the inadequacy of the form of life in civil society that such a Church presupposes and represents.

The implication of Douglas' work would seem to be, then, that we shall not get back an authentic liturgical life until we recover a rightly ordered society on the level both of the family, the microsociety, and of macrosociety, society at large. A "rightly ordered society" in this context is one that gives due place to common life, hierarchy, and shared authoritative public doctrine as well as to personal freedom and creativity. Here we can recall how for David Martin it is the error of the ideology of spontaneity not to realize that the second set of

[35] Ibid., 166.

these terms positively requires the first. If this thought, that liturgical malaise will not be fully rectified until a Christian society is reinstituted, seems somewhat daunting, we can turn for counterbalance to a last British anthropologist, Victor Turner, who appears to allow a greater autonomy or shaping power to what he calls in the title of a major book "the ritual process".[36]

In Turner's view, traditional liturgy, precisely because of its archaic quality, has a power to modify and even reverse the assumptions made in secular living.

> If ritual is not to be merely a reflection of secular social life, if its function is partly to protect and partly to express truths which make men free from the exigencies of their status-incumbencies, free to contemplate and pray as well as to speculate and invent, then its repertoire of liturgical actions should not be limited to a direct reflection of the contemporary scene.[37]

Insisting that the archaic is not the obsolete, Turner maintains that, on the contrary, archaic patterns of action are necessary to protect what he calls "future free spaces".

[36] V. Turner, *The Ritual Process: Structure and Anti-Structure* (Ithaca, 1969); also relevant is idem, *Dramas, Fields and Metaphors: Symbolic Action in Human Society* (Ithaca, 1974).

[37] V. Turner, "Passages, Margins and Poverty: Religious Symbols of *Communitas*", *Worship* 46 (1972): 391.

In this perspective he finds the de facto liturgical reform of the 1960s and 1970s somewhat incongruous. The reformers failed to appreciate the need of believers for repetition and archaism. He would not have appreciated the emphasis of Archbishop Annibale Bugnini, in his chronicle of the reform, on the "effort to make the rites speak the language of our own time",[38] even though Bugnini wrote his exhaustive account from a commanding height as secretary of the commission for liturgical reform established by Pius XII in 1948; secretary of the preparatory commission on the Liturgy at the Second Vatican Council (1960–1962); *peritus* of that Council and its commission on the Liturgy; secretary of the Concilium for the implementation of the Constitution on the Liturgy (1964–1969); and secretary of the Congregation for Divine Worship (1969–1975). Like Flanagan later, Turner held that pastoral liturgists were intimidated by the reigning "structural functionalism" in sociology. For that school, just as ritual structure reflects social structure, so ritual should change as society changes. Turner's own anthropological scheme, by contrast, privileges significant intervals where we cross what he calls *limina* (thresholds) in our passage *between* social experiences.

---

[38] A. Bugnini, *The Reform of the Liturgy,* 1948–1975 (Collegeville, Minn., 1990), 45.

In so doing, we periodically find ourselves separated from our statistically normal experience of identification with some limited group and enter at least for a while a state of what he terms *communitas,* a form of sociability where our capacity for identification with others is unrestricted by space, time, and even their biological dying, and we enter the experiential continuum he names "flow". Typically, ritual stands out from mundane culture in its use of a high language that abounds in lexical and grammatical forms no longer current in everyday speech. Optimally, ritual is a symphony of expressive genres, rather as opera works simultaneously through a multiplicity of art forms in prose and poetry, music and acting. Unlike opera, however, ritual escapes theatricality by the seriousness of its ultimate concerns.

In principle, what Turner says could be applied to the ritual activity of any society, Christian or not, in its religious dimension, and indeed his ideas were in part formulated through fieldwork among the Ndembu in Zambia. But in his essay "Ritual, Tribal and Catholic", Turner applies these notions more especially to the Western Mass.

> The traditional liturgy displayed an essential concern for proper form in the representation of sacred mysteries and the performance of symbolic acts. This was the fruit of popular wisdom fertilized by

developing doctrine, and shaped by esthetic as well
as legalistic principle. Ritual traditions of any depth
or complexity represent the consolidated understanding of many generations. They embody a deep
knowledge of the nature of flow, and how and where
to break it in order to instill truths about the nature
of time, the human condition, and evil. They reveal
an understanding of the religious benefit of flow as
much for individuals in their interior meditations
as for eliciting the spirit of communitas, or shared
flow, in congregations at worship.

And he continues:

A complete liturgical system represents an orga-
nised system of spiritual and rational achievements.
It is a work of ages, not a hackwork of contemporane-
ous improvisation. In its multiplicity and variety
(controlled, nevertheless, by hard-won rules), it
exemplifies the many-faceted yet single spirit of
mankind at prayer, of *homo religiosus.* Although
each nacreous increment which composes this pearl
has been laid down at a particular time, the total
liturgy is liberated from historical determinations.
When men and women enter the "liminality", the
tract of sacred space-time, which is made available
to them by such a traditional liturgy, they cease
to be bound by the secular structures of their own
age, and confront eternity which is equidistant from
all ages.[39]

[39] V. Turner, "Ritual, Tribal and Catholic", *Worship* 50 (1976):
523–24.

Whereas, so Turner pessimistically proposes, the "flow" elicited by the reformed Liturgy too often "bubbles on the surface" as a "transient communication".

A motif running through all these authors is the claim that the theological strategy of cultural modernism is misconceived. Modernism—I use the word in the sense of an intellectual style, not that of a heresy in the doctrine of revelation—is too indebted to those features of the Enlightenment and Romanticism that set those movements at odds with the Catholic Church or at any rate presented obstacles (as well as, to some extent, opportunities) for an authentic ecclesial reform and renewal. In the realm of liturgiology, if the eighteenth- and early-nineteenth-century discussion of liturgical revision had been better known and its lessons more fully pondered, if the foundational principles suggested by Trapp and shared by such leaders of the interwar liturgical movement as Casel and Guardini had been consistently applied to contemporary sensibility in the 1960s and 1970s, much harm might have been avoided. As it was, and despite the wonderful erudition liturgical scholars brought to the remaking of the rites, liturgists, in Flanagan's words, "managed to back modernity as a winning ticket, just at the point when it became converted into post-modernism".[40]

This statement at least makes the point that there is now nothing particularly modern about cultural modernism. It may also be interpreted as hinting that the postmodernist phase into which, in literary theory, philosophy, and a wider sensibility, a signifi-cant portion of the Western intelligentsia has now passed could have formed a happier context in which both to transmit and in various discreet and pru-dent ways to enhance a traditional rite.

Statements of what postmodernism is are gener-ally both elliptic and obscure, so much so that ques-tions of how precisely it differs from modernism, what intellectual virtues it recommends, and whether it contains, at least implicitly, any broad truth-claims about the nature of reality are, at least for the present writer, unanswered. But let me mention on the basis of recent research at Cambridge some ways in which one liturgist writing in a confessedly postmodernist manner would find neglected resources in a tradi-tional rite. Catherine Pickstock, of Emmanuel Col-lege, Cambridge, in her analysis of the old Roman eucharistic rite, stresses the mobile character of the liturgical "I", the self that worships. In liturgical action, I am not simply and in straightforward fash-

---

[40] Flanagan, *Sociology and Liturgy,* 42.

ion myself: hence the inappropriateness of attempting to fit the Liturgy to the needs of the extraliturgical personality, to make liturgy "relevant" to the ordinary persona of the self. Commenting on the Fore-Mass of the 1962 Missal, from the prayers of preparation to the Gloria, Pickstock writes:

> By means of its dispossessed and impersonating character, its taking on of the roles of other characters thereby unsettling the claim to a secure poetic voice, the worshipping I is designated by the act of forgetting itself, by the forgetting of ordinary identity.[41]

And again:

> This complex assuming of different voices leads to an interlacing of voices or polyphony at whose centre [here she refers to the opening of the Gloria] are the seraphic voices which are heard, alluded to, and intermingled with the human voices.[42]

Impersonation, she stresses, "precedes an authentic voice": that is, our Christian persona is formed by the way an extraliturgical sense of the "I" is modified and extended by the Liturgy itself. "This is a decentred 'I' which constantly moves from one identity to another, from immanent to transcendent

---

[41] C. Pickstock, "The Sacred Polis: Language, Death and Liturgy" (Ph.D. thesis, Cambridge, 1996), 195.

[42] Ibid., 203.

locations, breaking the quarantining of the two worlds, but without ever compromising their difference."[43] In a pithy axiom: "In giving (doxologically) we become (ontologically)." In other words, by worship our Christian selves are forged; so worship is not to be judged by what our secular or nonliturgical identity may desire or demand.

In her critique of the reform of the Roman rite, Pickstock argues that criticisms of the mediaeval Liturgy by conventional historians of the rite such as Theodor Klauser are misplaced.[44] For Klauser the repetitious and sometimes seemingly random structure of the preconciliar rite (one thinks especially of the often attacked Offertory prayers) bears witness to a debasement of pure Liturgy, as does the

[43] Ibid., 205.

[44] T. Klauser, *A Short History of the Western Liturgy,* 2d ed. (Oxford, 1979). One may add to Klauser's name that of the Italian liturgiologist influential in the drafting of the new anaphoras, Dom Cyprian Vagaggini, for whom the historic Roman Canon is disunified and illogical: "hardly a model of simplicity and clarity", *The Canon of the Mass and Liturgical Reform* (London, 1967), 96. But note the criticism of these criticisms by the Anglican liturgiologist Geoffrey Willis, who wrote that they may arise from a "failure to understand the processes by which the Roman *Canon Missae* reached its present form and even a failure to apprehend the basic principles of its structure": "The New Eucharistic Prayers: Some Comments", in *A Voice for All Time: Essays on the Liturgy of the Catholic Church since the Second Vatican Council,* ed. C. Francis and M. Lynch (Bristol, 1994), 91.

concomitant emphasis on purification and requests for mercy. Pickstock, on the other hand, treats a certain randomness and repetitiveness as reassuring signs of the oral provenance of the Roman Liturgy, intrinsic aspects of a flow typical of speech rather than a written structure whose meanings are "spatially" compartmentalized in discrete sections. In similar fashion, she takes the repeated requests for purification as signs of an underlying apophaticism that stresses our distance from God, not just our sinfulness, and emphasizes what she calls "the need for a constant re-beginning of liturgy because the true eschatological liturgy is in time endlessly postponed".[45] That early fourth-century text so important for the makers of the reformed Roman rite, the *Paradôsis apostolikê,* or *Apostolic Tradition,* ascribed to Hippolytus, being as it is more of a treatise on Liturgy than a Liturgy itself, proved misleading, she thinks, for the program of liturgical recovery, not least in these respects.

Rather like Douglas, Pickstock holds that to reform an ancient Liturgy successfully in radical guise would ultimately entail remaking the entire social order, for earlier Liturgies formed part of a culture itself ritual in character. What the Church could have done, however, was to refrain from assimilating

[45] Pickstock, "The Sacred Polis", 166.

"linguistic and structural forms" from modernity, for these are precisely the elements most inimical to liturgical goals. The "clear and linear purpose" of modern Liturgy is, in her view, sadly of this age of the world and hence in its connotations immanent when compared with traditional rites she character- izes as "a liturgical stammer in the face of the sub- lime excess of God".

For a Catholic Christian, in matters of the mind illumined by grace it is theology — sound and solid theology, drawn from Scripture and tradition under the guidance of the Magisterium — that is the queen of the sciences and not the cultural sciences that the writers whose ideas I have been rehearsing represent. That is not to say, however, that these benevolent warning voices can safely be disregarded. On the basis of her bimillennial experience, the Church has in the past been credited by sympathetic observers with a definite store of human wisdom. Like her divine Founder, she has known what is in man. The largely independent and convergent testimony of the men and women whose work I have described in this chapter suggests that of late the Church, which must mean here her members, has shown an unchar- acteristic deficiency of such wisdom, in part in the conception of the liturgical reform, but even more in its execution. This is something the clergy and laity of the next century will eventually need to address.

III

THE IDIOM OF WORSHIP

One of the founders of Christian sociology in England, and a major contributor to T. S. Eliot's Christendom Group, Canon Vigo Demant of Christ Church, Oxford, once remarked, "When the Church begins to proclaim the Gospel in a secular idiom she may end by proclaiming secularism in a Christian idiom".[1] "Idiom", of course, can mean different things. It may mean conceptual idiom, the doctrines or lack of them we appeal to in our preaching. Then again, it may mean linguistic idiom, as in the translation of the Bible for liturgical reading and of the prayers of the Liturgy themselves. It may be musical idiom, in the chants, hymns, and songs. It may be iconographic and architectural idiom, the visual setting of the liturgical action. All of these,

[1] Cited in P. W. Hoon, *The Integrity of Worship: Ecumenical and Pastoral Studies in Liturgical Theology* (Nashville and New York, 1971), 9.

unfortunately, can take desacralized, secularized forms and thus be rendered vulnerable to the operation of Demant's Law.

Thus in architectural matters, we often seem to be deaf to the language of sacred architecture in the Catholic tradition and mute to use it ourselves when a new church needs to be built. Our modern churches lack transcendence, the sense of mystery and beauty, the ability to inspire awe. Just as pastoral Liturgy fell victim, if we can believe Victor Turner, to structural functionalism in sociology, so for the last forty years Catholic architecture has been dominated by the school of thought known as "radical functionalism" as well. The symbolic aspect is to be left to itself so long as a building is "well ordered" for parish Liturgy. As Steven Schloeder has put it, architects

> have fallen into a reductionist mentality, stripping the churches of those elements, symbols and images that speak silently to the human heart. Their buildings speak only of the immanent—even as their liturgies studiously avoid the transcendent to dwell on the "gathered assembly"—and thus have departed from the theological and anthropological underpinnings of the traditional understanding of Catholic Church architecture. They have forgotten, or chosen to ignore, that religion necessarily points beyond itself.[2]

[2] S. Schloeder, "What Happened to Church Architecture", *Second Spring,* March 1995, 29.

Not only by virtue of its dedication but also because of the purposive Christian intelligence of its builders, a church should be a vehicle of grace for those properly disposed to dwell in it. It should be a symbolization via the properly architectural means of mass and space, shape and fabric, of the heavenly realities that surround the Liturgy of the throne of God to which the earthly Liturgy gives entrance. The postconciliar *Ordo dedicandi ecclesiae et altaris,* last of the texts of the reformed Liturgy, still retains this fundamental symbolism. What has not been realized, however, is that the ideas that underpin the Modern Movement in twentieth-century architecture, beginning with the German Bauhaus of the 1920s, and, along with these, the Modernist understanding of architectural language, simply cannot be combined with the Catholic tradition's own approach to church construction. Functional modernism is per se aniconic, indeed anti-iconic. In the modernist vocabulary, a door, for instance, is simply that. It cannot address the pregnant processes of entering, crossing thresholds, transition, and passage and therefore cannot speak, as in the mediaeval period it did to Durandus and Abbot Suger of St. Denis (authors of important treatises on building) of the person of Christ. Similarly, to the architectural modernist, space is essentially an empty universal, determined only by the function occurring in it at some time. There is no "sacred space", no space that is unconditionally set apart. Hence the possibility of modernist churches with multifunctional spaces usable indifferently for worship, wedding receptions, and playing table tennis. But a nonsymbolic building cannot, even with the best will in the world, communicate transcendent ideas.[3]

One particularly controverted point in this connection concerns the issue of the eastward orientation of church, altar, and celebration, or, more widely, of the *versus populum* over against the *versus apsidem* position. It seems undeniable that the weight of patristic scholarship is now placed on the side of the view that eastward orientation and so, generally

---

[3] The flawed pastoral strategy underlying such architectural options is (inadvertently) well expressed in the preface contributed to J. Capellades, *Guide des églises nouvelles de France* (Paris, 1969), by the then president of the French national committee for church building, who declared that as not only places of assembly for Catholics but also places of welcome and contact with separated Christians or simply men of good will, churches should have no style of their own, "since forms that would wish to break with present-day architecture risk signifying the noncontemporariness [*inactualité*] of the Church". Cited in G. Cholmy and Y. M. Hilaire, "1968: Les Institutions contestées. Une institution dépassée: la paroisse?", in idem, *Histoire contemporaine de la France religieuse, 1930–1968* (Toulouse, 1988), 318.

speaking, *versus apsidem* celebration was the norm in the early Church. In his paper "*Eis anatolas blepsete: Orientation as a Liturgical Principle*", published in *Studia Patristica* for 1982, Canon M. J. Moreton of Exeter University has gathered together the most important extant data, whether textual or architectural, on this subject.[4] At Dura-Europos, the ancient Mesopotamian riverine city, with its significant Christian and Jewish communities, one of the best preserved synagogues of late antiquity and the only house church of the pre-Nicene period to have survived lie in close proximity. But while the first is orientated toward Jerusalem, the second is orientated in the strict sense of that word—aligned with the east. As Moreton comments:

> In this respect we encounter at Dura for the first time a conflict of principle which goes to the heart of what is at issue between Judaism and Christianity, viz., whether the advent of the Messiah is still future or already realized; whether it is looked for in the devout observance of the Torah, itself associated with the land, the city and the Temple in Jerusalem, or realized in the performance of the Liturgy.[5]

[4] M. J. Moreton, "*Eis anatolas blepsete:* Orientation as a Liturgical Principle", in *Studia Patristica* 18, ed. E. A. Livingstone (Oxford and New York, 1982), 575–90.

[5] Ibid., 578.

In time, indeed, the messianic salutation *Benedictus qui venit in nomine Domini!* would displace a Jewish benedictus verse referring to that temple as the regular accompaniment to the liturgical Sanctus, telling as the latter originally did in its biblical context of the prophet Isaiah's temple vision. In the consecratory prayers of a variety of Eastern anaphora (the Liturgy of the Twelve Apostles, the Liturgy of Saint James, the Liturgy of Saint Basil, the Liturgy of Saint John Chrysostom), this marks the point where reference to God's work in creation is replaced by an account of his work in Jesus Christ. So contextualized, the orientation of the church building in which the Liturgy is performed "expresses the hope and confidence of the Church in him whose coming was from the East in the historic past, and will be again at the glorious Parousia"[6] the Eucharist as efficacious memorial of the one and anticipation of the other joining the two in the present.

Of course this would be overinterpretation were the Dura case isolated. That Dura-Europos is *not* fortuitous, however, is demonstrated by comparison with the orientation of the numerous churches of the fourth to seventh centuries that have left their trace in Syria and Palestine. With few exceptions, the disposition of furniture, especially the altar and

[6] Ibid., 583.

the *synthronon* (the stone bench where the presby-
ters sat), assumes that the clergy occupied the entrance to the nave for the Liturgy of the Word but
proceeded for the Eucharistic Liturgy proper to an
altar lying deep within the apse, if not indeed bonded
to its rear wall. In Constantinople, centrally orga-
nized and domed churches follow the principle of
orientation no less than do the very different Syro-
Palestinian basilicas. Though the *synthronon* in the
early Constantinopolitan churches is situated in the
apse, altars were sited over a centrally positioned
crypt allowing access only from the west side — once
again requiring the celebrant, like the congregation,
to face eastward. In Christian North Africa, the
basilica with an eastern apse was the norm in all
periods, although in the fourth and fifth centuries
(but not later) some Tunisian churches have, excep-
tionally, their apses in the west, whence the clergy
would look out toward not only their congregation
but also a centrally placed altar. It seems likely that
these atypical churches were constructed on the
model of the Lateran basilica, itself patterned on
the palatine architecture of the imperial audience
hall, where the emperor or his representative sat in
the west. An occidental apse does not of itself,
however, prove the incidence of *versus populum*
celebration. Given the fact that the faithful stood in
two great swathes to the north and south of the nave,

it is conceivable that everyone present, people and celebrant, turned to face the east, the doors of the church, when the Liturgy of the Sacrifice began. At any rate, the example of the *Laterana* was insufficient to affect the sanctuaries of that other most influential portion of the Roman "diocese" (along with North Africa), northern Italy, where the churches of Milan and Ravenna kept strictly to the principle of orientation.

But where, then, did the idea of celebration *versus populum* come from on a grand scale? Almost certainly from two crucial buildings that, paradoxically, were not designed for the celebration of the Liturgy at all: the rotunda of the Church of the Anastasis at Jerusalem and the martyrium of Saint Peter's in Rome. In each case constraints of site and space and the prestige of the sacred spot — the site of the Resurrection in the one case, the last resting place of the prince of the apostles in the other — legitimized an anomaly. Although such "opposing of celebrant and faithful" (in Moreton's phrase) "ran counter to the tradition of prayer toward the east which was deeply founded in Christian practice", the prestige of Saint Peter's in the West, reinforced by *ad limina* pilgrimage as this was, resulted eventually in many other Western churches following this example, though lacking, as Jocelyn Toynbee and John Ward Perkins remark in their study of the shrine of Saint Peter, the same compelling reason for doing so.[7]

Actually, if we survey the Western rite tradition as a whole we find, as Father Jaime Lara has shown in a fascinating article in *Worship,* a remarkable inventiveness.[8] While westward *versus populum* celebration is relatively rare and usually derives from a desire to do all things *more romano,* following the example of Saint Peter's and the basilicas that took up the cue from the Vatican Hill, other possibilities have also been explored. There have been *altaria superiora,* as in certain Carolingian churches and some Anglo-Norman cathedrals, where the altar was located above the faithful on a balcony. Or again the altar has been below them as at Aachen, where the bulk of the congregation was housed, with the emperor, in a great gallery. Yet again there is the arrangement depicted in the anonymous sixteenth-century painting "The Mass of St. Giles", in the National Gallery in London, where the faithful peep out around the curtains or from behind the retable of an eastward-facing altar.

Recently the Congregation for Divine Worship

[7] J. Toynbee and J. Ward Perkins, *The Shrine of St. Peter* (London, 1956), 219.

[8] J. Lara, "Versus Populum Revisited", *Worship* 68, no. 3 (1994): 210–21.

has admitted that eastward orientation, not *versus populum* celebration, is the tradition in possession in the Church viewed diachronically, across time.[9] In that sense the *onus probandi* falls on those who would justify an alternative siting. Of course justification exists: whether material, as in the impediment of the *confessio* tomb and its little window for relic-gazing and lowering down objects as at Saint Peter's, or spiritual, as in the case made in the Catholic Student Movement in the Germany of the 1930s or the worker-priest movement in the France of the 1950s. It must be borne in mind, however, that the roots of the pressure for *versus populum* celebration in the modern liturgical movement lie in the soil of the eighteenth-century Enlightenment, where they are hard to disentangle from a conscious effort to divert attention away from the Eucharist as sacrifice—a term as opaque to rationalistically inclined Catholics then as to many of our contemporaries now—and toward the much more comprehensible notions of the Eucharist as assembly and as meal. In a personal reminiscence, I recall the vicar of Tewkesbury (Gloucestershire) telling me in 1969, when my own home was some few miles up the Severn, that for High Anglicans like himself the abandonment of *versus apsidem* celebration was unthinkable, since it was part-and-parcel of their strug-

[9] In *Notitiae* 29, no. 332 (1993): 245–49.

gle to revive a sense of the Eucharist as sacrifice in the Church of England. But for Roman Catholics, he thought, *versus populum* celebration would do no harm. Our sense of the Sacrifice of the Mass was too deep to be shaken. This was too kindly a view of the capacity of the contemporary *sensus fidei,* at any rate in England.

Today the question should be determined, in my judgment, in relation to the threat of what we can call "cultic immanentism": the danger, namely, of a congregation's covert self-reference in a horizontal, humanistic world. In contemporary "Catholic communalism", it has been said: "Liturgical *Gemütlichkeit,* communal warmth, friendliness, welcoming hospitality, can easily be mistaken for the source and summit of the faith."[10] Not unconnected with this is the possibility that the personality of the priest (inevitably, as president, the principal facilitator of such a therapeutic support-group) will become the main ingredient of the whole ritual. Unfortunately, the "liveliest church in town" has little to do with the life the Gospel speaks of.

Henri de Lubac wrote in *The Splendor of the Church:*

> In the present welcome efforts to bring about a celebration of the liturgy which is more "communal"

[10] T. Day, *Where Have You Gone, Michelangelo? The Loss of Soul in Catholic Culture* (New York, 1993), 107.

and more alive, nothing would be more regrettable than a preoccupation with the success achieved by some secular festivals by the combined resources of technical skill and the appeal to man at his lower level. . . . The "unanimous life of the Church" is not a natural growth; it is lived through faith; our unity is the fruit of Calvary, and results from the Mass's application to us of the merits of the Passion, with a view to our final redemption.[11]

De Lubac glimpsed in fact a nightmare prospect that the Church, by misjudged benevolence, could realize Auguste Comte's prediction that Catholicism would find its last end in an apotheosis of humanity. Detecting a "growing homogeneity between worshippers and the beings that are worshipped", Comte envisaged the Church as making a significant contribution to the long process of immanentization that, he hoped, would terminate in the simultaneous elimination of God and deification of man. The dogma of the Incarnation, Comte thought, would see its final fruit in an ecclesiology where the Church becomes the sacrament of humanity, itself the one and only true Supreme Being. And de Lubac comments:

We should not be too quick to cry out in protest, as if there were never any danger of anything like

[11] H. de Lubac, S.J., *The Splendor of the Church* (San Francisco, 1986), 155–56.

that in ourselves. . . . No sincere Christian will go so far as to profess a "sociological pantheism"; but that is not to say that everyone will always, both in his emotional reactions and his practical conduct, be effectively strengthened in advance against the present tendency to absorb God into the human community.[12]

Recalling Torquemada's criticism of the Council of Basel for allowing its members to genuflect when they sang the article of the Creed concerning the Church, de Lubac concludes that a shift in our focus of interest can sometimes symptomize a doctrinal debilitation and hollowness far graver than more obvious errors. I suggest that the concentration on congregation and presider in contemporary eucharistic practice is an example of just such debilitation and hollowness, unfortunately encouraged by the *versus populum* celebration of the Eucharistic Prayer.

If our worship, then, is in need of new openness to transcendence, or, to put the same point in a more distinctively Christian way, if God's self-identification in Jesus Christ is what shall determine worship in his Name, this should be achieved not primarily by direct exhortation, which belongs chiefly to kerygmatic preaching and catechesis, but by specifically ritual means proper to the Liturgy itself. And these will include not only architectural setting and the

[12] Ibid., 226–27.

disposition of priest and people in relation to the
altar within that setting but also, in the *Gesamtkunstwerk* (as Richard Wagner might have called it)—the
total artwork—of the Liturgy, language and music
as well.

In his wise and distinctly against-the-stream study
The Integrity of Worship, the American Protestant
theologian of liturgy Paul Whitman Hoon points
out:

> While we must be always aware of the seduction
> of Liturgy into art for art's sake, it must be recognised
> that man engages more readily in the dialogue of
> worship when its forms please his sensibilities at the
> same time as they are appropriate to the majesty of
> God.[13]

And he adds in this connection: "Forms which at
first sight seem to offend by their archaism often
possess prototypical power to engage man's deepest
nature which familiar forms do not."[14] What is different makes us sit up. George Kennedy, in his study
of the rhetoric of the early Christian Liturgy, has
described what he calls the "pull . . . toward the exotic
as a feature of sacral language". Though for Augustine
the old Latin Bible with its unnatural rhythms
and queer metaphors was distinctly offputting, and

---

[13] Hoon, *Integrity of Worship*, 41.
[14] Ibid., 42.

Kennedy notes that it was not the Liturgy of the Milanese church that triggered Augustine's conversion but Ambrose's allegorical expositions of the Scriptures in the homilies, others appear to have reacted differently. Kennedy suggests that the development of a linguistic sacrality with its own power began in the Church as early as the reception of the Septuagint. As he writes:

> Unusual meanings are given to Greek words to approximate to the Hebrew; the imagery of the psalms and prophets, though largely comprehensible, overreaches and strains Greek metaphorical conventions, and the result seems oriental, bizarre, but also suggestive of divine inspiration. God would not necessarily speak in ordinary language, and perhaps this language is his. The language both veils and partially reveals truths too great for direct human utterance.[15]

And he concludes by pointing out that features thus associated with the inspiration of the Septuagint text were then imitated in the Christian preaching and prayer that were that text's extended vehicles. Reminding his readers how that outstanding student of patristic language Christine Mohrmann had described the whole of the earliest eucharistic termi-

---

[15] G. Kennedy, "The Rhetoric of the Early Christian Liturgy", in *Language and the Worship of the Church,* ed. D. Jasper and R. C. D. Jasper (London, 1990), 36.

nology in Greek as "deliberately isolated from the
language of everyday life", Kennedy remarks wryly
that "the modern liturgists who would like to view
the earliest eucharistic celebration as a 'gathering
round the kitchen table' certainly do not find support in the testimony of [that] earliest terminology."[16]
The language of the Liturgy is of course human, yet
the kinds of communication aimed at transcend ordinary human notions of how language is purpose-
fully used.

There is an argument here either for the reten-
tion of an otherwise unusual sacral language (Latin,
Church Slavonic, premodern Greek) or for the preservation of a relatively archaic and high version of
the vernacular, marking off a difference from secular language use. Dr. R. H. Richens, the Cambridge
botanist and musician who founded the Association
for the Latin Liturgy, has in mind both these options,
but with a bias to the first (at any rate in the local
churches primarily indebted to European civilization), when he writes

> The tendency to exalt the role of simple commu-
> nication in dealing with sacred texts is extremely
> dangerous, since it leads so easily to the fatal miscon-
> ception that the divine mysteries are now explained.
> This is the penultimate stage to explaining them

[16] Ibid., 37; cf. C. Mohrmann, *Liturgical Latin, Its Origins and
Character* (Washington, 1957), 25–26.

away, to conceiving divine and human understanding as of the same nature, and thus ultimately to obliterating the gulf between the infinite and the finite. Atheism follows quite logically. One of the most effective counter-balances to this tendency is to use numinous language in which the words, while communicating their message, remind us of the infinity of being lying beyond. It need hardly be added that the sacral languages of the ancient liturgies . . . have this numinous quality in pre-eminent degree.[17]

The word "numinous" is a difficult one, but we might paraphrase it as "imbued with religious gravity". So far as the vernacular is concerned, it has been well said of, for instance, Cranmer's "General Confession for Holy Communion", dependent as this was on a Latin original, that "one does not have to be a good actor to bring out at once its sense and its gravity."[18]

And yet of course the Roman rite is essentially a *chanted* rite, and so we need not and should not think of the word here as wholly unsupported by music. From the Guéranger phase of the liturgical

[17] R. H. Richens, "Latin Liturgy and Christian Credibility", in *A Voice for All Time: Essays on the Liturgy of the Catholic Church since the Second Vatican Council,* ed. C. Francis and M. Lynch (Bristol, 1994), 133.

[18] P. Mack, "Rhetoric and Liturgy", in *Language and the Worship of the Church,* 103.

movement onward, conventionally dated as that phase is to the publication of the first volume of *L'Année liturgique* in 1840, the recovery of a more fully authentic liturgical life in the West was inseparable, until recent decades, from concern with the chant. After Guéranger had set his scholars to work, and notably Dom Pothier and Dom Mocquereau, the revelation of the chant's qualities inspired Pope Pius X to issue his 1903 *motu proprio* on sacred music, which was called by the Lutheran historian of the Catholic liturgical movement Ernest Koenker "the fundamental musical directive of the Liturgical Movement, the great musical document in Roman Catholic Church history".[19] Although Pius X did not restrict sacred music to Gregorian, he insisted that the qualities that should always typify such music — holiness, goodness of form, universality — were preeminently embodied there. Just as Leo XIII had found the desiderata of a Catholic theology classically embodied in Thomas, though not everyone need be a Thomist, so Pius X saw Gregorian chant as the classical or paradigmatic music of the Church, though it need not be exclusively performed. Still, to serve as a paradigm, the "classic" must of course be available, known, and used. Hence the

[19] E. Koenker, *The Liturgical Renaissance in the Roman Catholic Church* (Chicago, 1954), 154.

unified pluralism proposed by the *motu proprio* is combined with a plea for the reinstatement of the classic form. As the Pope put it:

> The more closely a Church composition approaches plain chant in movement, inspiration, and feeling, the more holy and liturgical it becomes; and the more out of harmony it is with this supreme model, the less worthy it is of the temple. Special efforts should be made to restore the use of Gregorian chant by the people so that the faithful may again take a more active part in the ecclesiastical offices, as was the case in ancient times.[20]

At any rate in England, and despite all the professed loyalty of the Catholic community of the time to the Holy See, the response was minimal until McElligott's inauguration of the Society of Saint Gregory in 1929, in the wake of Pius XI's *Divini Cultus,* which reiterated his predecessor's stand but now in the more authoritative guise, for those sensitive to such protocols, of an "Apostolic Constitution".[21] After that, positively Herculean efforts were made, especially through a useful précis of the repertoire, *Plainsong for Schools,* whose first volume, published in 1933, sold over one hundred thousand

---

[20] *"Motu proprio" on Sacred Music* (Conception, Mo., 1945), 5–6.

[21] J. Ainslie, "English Liturgical Music before Vatican II", in *English Catholic Worship: Liturgical Renewal in England since 1900,* ed. J. D. Crichton et al. (London, 1979), 47–59.

copies over a period of eighteen months. There were regional festivals, too, and the Society's own summer schools. Though momentum was somewhat lost after World War II, partly owing to new and improved non-Gregorian settings of the Ordinary as well as *Mediator Dei*'s permission for vernacular hymns at Low Mass, the capacity crowds of two thousand and more who in the years 1937 to 1939 at Westminster Cathedral sang the *Ordinarium Missae* from the *Kyriale* (and not the *Missa de Angelis* either!) with a schola of male amateurs rendering the *Proprium Missae* remain in the corporate memory as testimonials to what could be done. The Second Vatican Council renewed the pledge of the early-twentieth-century popes to the chant and to the polyphony that can be regarded as the authentic continuation of its qualities in the specifically choral tradition, but to no avail. The scores of the chant books and polyphonic settings were cleared out of the choir lofts and dumped in used bookstores, where astute entrepreneurs were more than willing to exploit them, having grasped (as one commentator has put it) their ability to comfort the afflicted.[22]

What has replaced the chant and polyphony does not bear too much thinking about,[23] though we

[22] Day, *Where Have You Gone*, 33.

[23] T. Day, *Why Catholics Can't Sing: The Culture of Catholicism and the Triumph of Bad Taste* (New York, 1990).

must admit that the vices of contemporary liturgical music were to some degree prepared in Anglo-Saxon lands by the deficiencies of at least one strand in the preconciliar hymnography. Writing in 1954, Koenker describes the favorite Catholic hymns in the United States as inducing "the same emotional 'jag' as popular love songs",[24] and yet Franck's *Panis Angelicus* and the Schubert *Ave Maria,* which he includes in this indictment, remain a cut above the way we live now.[25] The fact is that, while serious concert music has been driven by its history farther and farther up an arid intellectual cul-de-sac, popular music has gone down a similar dead end, but one situated at the opposite extreme, because governed by raw emotion, the outflow of untreated feeling. The synthesis of intellectual and emotional content that good music should always possess, and which could be taken for granted not only in high art but even in

---

[24] Koenker, *Liturgical Renaissance,* 154.

[25] The reinvigoration of vernacular hymnography by the removal from modern Catholic hymnals of hymns either lacking in or misrepresenting doctrinal content should be a priority. For the role of hymnography in the struggle against religious subjectivism, rationalism, and moralism, see the two heroic examples, one Lutheran, the other Anglican, described in L. Litvack, "The Greek Hymn Translations and Adaptations of N. F. S. Grundvig and J. M. Neale", *Hymn Society of Great Britain and Ireland Bulletin* 12, no. 10 (1990): 182–87; and idem, *John Mason Neale and the Quest for Sobornost* (Oxford, 1994), 94–101.

much folk art in previous centuries, is now extraordinarily hard to find. Hence the régime to which, by insistence that a modern Liturgy requires the use of contemporary media, we have been forcibly submitted. Thomas Day has described it to perfection as a diet of romantic marshmallows indigestibly combined with "stuff that grabs you by the scruff of the neck and shakes you into submission with its social · message".[26] John Ainslie, formerly secretary of the Society of Saint Gregory but far from a traditionalist in matters of liturgy at large, commented in 1979, after a decade of experience:

> What was the rationale of such music? Many well-intentioned nuns, teachers and later priests thought that such "folk music" would appeal to teenagers and young people generally and so encourage them to participate in the Liturgy instead of walk out from it. The term "folk music" is, of course, misleading. There is nothing, for example, to link it with the English folk-song tradition, whatever that may be and even though it may be dead. The name was no doubt coined partly because some of the early repertoire was imported from the United States, where it *might* have been called folk music with some justification, partly because it was felt that the style had something in common with the musical tastes of today's younger generation and with their sub-culture. But it has never been persuasively shown

[26] Day, *Where Have You Gone,* 169.

that whatever young people may find attractive to listen to in a disco (or perhaps to participate in by "dancing"), they will find attractive to sing in church. Further, the style is unsuitable for singing by large congregations without at least as much practice as the singing of a new plainsong Mass . . . in former times — more so if the only accompaniment provided is a guitar rather than the organ, since guitars, even amplified, have insufficient "bite" to keep a whole congregation singing together and to give them the support they have come to expect from the organ.[27]

Moreover, whereas "traditional" (English Victorian) vernacular hymns integrate tolerably well with formal liturgy, the hail-fellow-well-met style of music and lyrics of liturgical folk music would require a different sort of Liturgy altogether — and that, of course, is what some people are only too willing to provide. In a recent survey of American liturgical composers, one of those interviewed, Father Jan Michael Joncas, described a Liturgy where events and texts are performed in the order laid down as only one possible option. Side by side with this "rubrical approach" are, Joncas explained, the "reflective approach", where "we begin with these liturgical books but the issue is not making sure these texts and ceremonies are done in this order but how

[27] J. Ainslie, "English Liturgical Music since the Council", in *English Catholic Worship*, 105.

they reflect the faith experience of the gathered community", and the "radical approach", which, he said, "tends not to pay attention to the liturgical books as published but begins with the spiritual experience of a given community and then tries to ritualize it".[28]

What we are witnessing here is not simply a secularization of the idiom of Christian worship (the issue raised by Demant) but the expropriation of the Liturgy from the Church altogether, in favor of its re-creation by particular groups that cannot claim to represent the *ekklêsiastikon phronêma*, the *sensus Ecclesiae.* Victor Turner wrote of the old Roman rite:

> One advantage of the traditional Latin ritual was that it could be performed by the most diverse groups and individuals, surmounting the divisions of age, sex, ethnicity, culture, economic status, or political affiliation. The liturgy stands out as a magnificent objective creation if the will to assist both lovingly and well was there. Now one fears that the tendentious manipulation of particular interest-groups is liquidating the ritual bonds which held the entire heterogeneous mystical body together in worship.[29]

[28] D. Gibeau, "Good Ritual Music Is a Complex Package", *The National Catholic Reporter,* May 12, 1995, 13.

[29] V. Turner, "Ritual, Tribal and Catholic", *Worship* 50 (1976): 525.

Nor is such instrumentalization of Liturgy for particular group-expressive purposes simply a narrowing down of the celebrating subject of the Mass, the mystical body. It is also a narrowing down of the objective scope of the celebration, which should be universal, cosmic in character. The Anglo-Welsh poet David Jones, in his *Anathemata,* takes as the context for his universal epic the consecration at the Western Mass, beginning with the elevation of the Host (the "efficacious sign", as Jones calls it) and closing with the elevation of the chalice (the "stemmed dish"). He makes of the Mass, as one critic has put it, "a complex of symbols capable of ordering and interpreting pretty well the whole of the history of the world and the whole order of nature".[30] The idea at the center of the *Anathemata* is that all distinctively human activity — the making of signs of whatever kind, the reshaping of the raw material of creation in humanly meaningful ways — finds its focus in the Mass. At the start of the poem, the celebrating presbyter appears as a craftsman, linked thus to the "makers" of prehistoric times, shaping and making other the bread and wine through the *prex sacerdotalis* so that they will not only be acceptable to God but also in a new way meaningful to

[30] B. Bunting, in a letter of April 18, 1979, cited in T. Dilworth, *The Shape of Meaning in the Poetry of David Jones* (Toronto, 1988), 5–6.

man. At the end of the poem, Christ is found plac-
ing himself in the order of signs in the Cenacle and
on Calvary, sacramentally identical as these are with
the Mass.

> He does what is done in many places,
>   what he does other
>   he does after the mode
>   of what has always been done.
> What did he do other
>   recumbent at the garnished supper?
> What did he do yet other
>   riding the Axile Tree?[31]

—the "axile tree", for the Cross is the true World
Tree prefigured in Norse mythology, the real axis
of the world, and now it is "ridden" by Christ as
Apollo rode the chariot of the sun. In giving the
Mass, as the crafted sign of this universal meaning
at the Supper, Christ did what men had always
done. They had always made signs and offered sacri-
fices in their worship. But he also "made it other".
He transformed it distinctively, indeed, he transub-
stantiated it. The poem closes as the triple exposure
of Supper, Calvary, and Mass resolves into the double
exposure of Last Supper and Mass and then into the
single image of the Mass today as the priest elevates

[31] D. Jones, *The Anathemata* (London, 1952; 1972), 243.

the chalice and completes the consecratory action underway moments before.[32] It is not perhaps surprising to find Jones' name as a signatory to the letter to the Holy See, published in *The Times* for July 6, 1971, sent to Rome by a number of writers, artists, and critics, not all of them Catholics, appealing for the preservation of the rite of the *Missale Pianum* on the grounds that it "belongs to universal culture as well as to churchmen and formal Christians".

A key word of Jones' vocabulary is the "utile", by which he means objects made with a view to mere utility, to him a subhuman project, to be contrasted with the making of things simultaneously useful and beautiful, which he saw as the characteristic activity of man. What we face today might be called the utilitarianization of worship, where worship is viewed chiefly as a means to effect changes in man and the human world, a return in fact of the discredited theology of Liturgy of the radical Enlightenment. But though the trinitarian God in the philanthropy he directs to man's salvation is never alone, his worship has nonetheless no moral or social purpose. It has meaning, a fullness of meaning, but

[32] T. Dilworth, *Poetry of David Jones*, 168. In interpreting this passage, I found helpful the exegesis offered by Father Bruce Harbert of Saint Mary's College, Oscott, in his "The Quest for Melchizedek", *New Blackfriars* 68, no. 810 (1987): 536–39.

to overlay it with a purpose is to destroy its nature.[33]
The Oxford philosopher of language J. L. Austin
asked: Is importance important? We might ask in
our context: Is relevance relevant? The Lutheran
theologian Paul Tillich, invited to contribute an
essay to a collection entitled *Making the Ministry
Relevant,* declared: "To point with inner authority
to the eternal is the most relevant function men
can perform today."[34] The "most relevant" because
human nature in all times and places, in whatever
sociological matrix or historical conjuncture, remains
a theotropic nature, as much made for communion
with the divine reality as the heliotrope, the sun-
flower, is drawn to the sun.

[33] Cf. V. Demant, "The Social Implications of Worship", in
Worship: Its Social Significance, ed. P. T. R. Kirk (London, 1939),
107–8.

[34] P. Tillich, "The Relevance of the Ministry in Our Time
and Its Theological Foundation", in *Making the Ministry Relevant,*
ed. H. Hofmann (New York, 1960), 35.

IV

A PRACTICAL CONCLUSION

I come now to the final question I must address, and that is the formulation of a practical policy. If we may borrow from a dictum of Marx, the point is not only to understand the Church; the point is (in this particular context) to change her. And so we have to ask in the words of a vastly influential pamphlet by Marx' not always faithful disciple Lenin, *Chto delat?*, What is to be done? Before endeavoring to answer this question, I note the power of words, to which, despite the characteristic emphasis of Marxism-Leninism, that pamphlet testified. The liturgical movement was itself, in its threefold nature as intellectual study, clerical reform, and lay education, essentially an affair of words. And so what words have done not altogether and in every respect well, words may presumably in some aspect undo, and do anew and better.

Our first task is, I am afraid, a negative one, namely, to prevent the further erosion of the liturgical patrimony of Western Catholicism, to forestall, that is, any further dose of reform in the same direction as that of the postconciliar one, though this be the medicine that some highly placed liturgists are determined to administer to us. I have in mind especially Dom Adrien Nocent's recently translated *Re-reading of the Renewed Liturgy,*[1] which proposes among other things the abbreviation on weekdays of the introductory rite to a simple greeting, so as to provide more time for the readings and a ten-minute (!) homily; the transfer of the *pax* to the beginning of the Offertory, and the suppression not only of the *lavabo* but also, more significantly still, of the elevations at the consecration. Dom Nocent, a cofounder of the Pontifical Liturgical Institute in Rome and writing with an almost Chinese punctiliousness of etiquette toward the mandarins of the Congregation for Divine Worship, suggests yet further options in the Lectionary cycle, the writing of original collects in all vernacular Liturgies since experience teaches that Latin concision cannot be replicated in other tongues, and reconstruction of and additions to the new Canons on the model of those Oriental anaphora that have only one epiclesis, *after* the words of consecration.

---

[1] A. Nocent, *A Re-reading of the Renewed Liturgy* (Collegeville, Minn., 1994).

I should not give the impression that Nocent's
entire project is misconceived. Some of his arguments—for instance, that, because the Roman Liturgy is essentially directed to the Father through
the Son in the Spirit, the eucharistic acclamation
after the words of institution should itself be directed
not to the Son but to the Father—seem fair enough.
And yet we might add that, considering the whole-
sale importation of Oriental-inspired Eucharistic
Prayers in the *Missale Paulinum* (for even the Prayer
of Hippolytus, Canon II, is considered by some
scholars to be non-Roman, indeed, non-Western),
this is rather rich: a clear case of shutting the stable
door after the horse has bolted! The elimination of
the Sanctus from the Second Eucharistic Prayer,
which Nocent also advocates on grounds of historical authenticity, would subtract from the Mass, when
celebrated with that Canon, a feature that has deeply
embedded itself in Catholic devotion since the early
Middle Ages. We are here in the midst of a veritable
building yard of that "fabricated liturgy" deplored
by Cardinal Ratzinger in his encomium on the
late Klaus Gamber of the Regensburg Liturgical
Institute.[2] The trouble is that, in the present situ-

[2] Published as a quasi preface to K. Gamber, *La Réforme
liturgique en question,* French trans. (Le Barroux, 1992), 6–8. Extracts
appear in the English version of this book: *The Reform of the
Roman Liturgy: Its Problems and Background* (San Juan Capistrano,
Calif., and Harrison, N.Y., 1993).

ation, even well-thought-out measures of further innovatory change in the rite will be met by incomprehension and indifference on the part of many and by irritation and anger on that of others, and, we must add, understandably so. Nonetheless it would probably be optimistic to suppose that none of the Nocent proposals (which also touch the sacraments of initiation and Penance) will strike any answering chord in the Roman dicastery.

Our next task is a more positive one: namely, the prayerful, dignified, correct, and, where appropriate, solemn celebration of the *Novus Ordo*. Here Msgr. Peter Elliott's recent provision of a rubrical directory for the Pauline Missal and other rites is helpful.[3] By the quality of Church fabrics and metals,[4] on the one hand, and of Church music,

---

[3] P. J. Elliott, *Ceremonies of the Modern Roman Rite: The Eucharist and the Liturgy of the Hours* (San Francisco, 1995).

[4] "Fabrics and metals": ideally, in the spirit of A. N. Pugin, by considering the church building as a whole, where not only painting, statuary, and furniture but also ceramic, metalwork, glass, textiles, books, and even jewelry (as in the crowns of Mother and Child at Saint Mary's, Oscott) cohere, bearing in mind the axiom stated in Pugin's *True Principles of Pointed or Christian Architecture* (London, 1841), that "all ornament should consist of enrichment of the essential construction of the building." Here the setting is as much *Gesamtkunstwerk* as is the Liturgy itself. See the essays in P. Atterbury and C. Wainwright, eds., *Pugin: A Gothic Passion* (New Haven and London, 1994). Yet strange stylistic juxtapositions can also work well. One thinks of the austere

on the other, much can be done to enhance the visual and aural setting of the Liturgy and to convey a sense of the supreme care and devotion with which it should be celebrated. The liturgically inept Jerusalem Bible Lectionary can be avoided, since copies of its Revised Standard Version competitor are still extant and make their occasional appearance in the second-hand catalogs of Catholic booksellers and can be bound and rebound until such time as the publisher be ready to risk re-issue. The liturgical strength of Latin can be invoked, at least in some sung parts of the Ordinary. Movement and gestures—of servers as well as of the officiating clergy— can be monitored. Extraordinary ministers of Holy Communion, if needed, can be suitably robed. Intrusive microphones can be removed from the sanctuary. Nor does anything in Church law prevent the recovery of the eastward or *versus apsidem* position (after due explanation to congregations!) for the recital of the Eucharistic Prayer.

But none of this will restore an adequate continuity with the textuality of the Roman rite in its earlier incarnation or with its ritual integrity as a unity of word and action. Here I would look instead to the

---

late Victorian liturgiologist Edmund Bishop's delight at the "characteristic super-imposition of baroque High Altars upon Gothic choirs" in Flanders: N. Abercrombie, *The Life and Work of Edmund Bishop* (London, 1959), 47.

provision by the Holy See of means for a future moderate revision of those earlier forms of the Latin rite that the Commission *Ecclesa Dei* was created to succor. It is for one thing obviously anomalous that rites exist that lack all provision for the amplification of their sanctorals when God gives his Church new saints. It is comprehensible that in the present climate, and given the wounds that years of turbulent Church history have inflicted on many, for those who have regained the privilege of canonical worship using the Pian Missal or analogues like the Dominican book in use in 1962, the last thing they will want to think about is liturgical revision. Yet the only way in which the wider Latin church can profit by the providential survival of these older forms of the Latin rite is through their reappropriation in modified guise.

In saying this, I have in mind not only the vernacular reading of Scripture in public worship, something already tending to replace Latin lections before the Council opened, but also: a resolution of the disparities between the 1969 Calendar and its predecessor; the enhancement of the range of Prefaces to be found in the 1962 books on the basis of the fine ones now found in the Pauline Missal; some augmentation of their Lectionary resources, though not on the system of a two- or three-year cycle, which destroys the integrated character of a liturgical day;

and, not least, the possibility of offering the chalice to the lay faithful when appropriate. All of these things would help the traditional rite to capitalize on the strong points of the postconciliar reform.

What, then, in my version of things, would happen to the Missal of 1969 itself? Given the fact that the Rite of Paul VI contains more features of Oriental provenance than the Roman rite has ever known historically (and notably in the new anaphoras, for these are central to the definition of any eucharistic style), I would propose its redesignation as *ritus communis,*[5] with a multiple purpose in view.

First, it could be used as a basis for the development of new ritual families in those parts of the universal Church that have a high culture of their own, worthy of providing a ritual house of gestures and poetry to enshrine the Mass. India is an obvious example. I am aware that the general proposition of new rites of the Mass for young churches with indigenous cultures far removed from the Semitic-Greco-Roman world of Bible and Fathers is

[5] Dr. Geoffrey Willis has spoken of a "general policy of revision which has shown itself prepared, and even anxious, to incorporate into the Western liturgy features which are not native to it, but confessedly derived from Oriental sources. . . . The rite has certainly become hybrid", "The New Eucharistic Prayers: Some Comments", in *A Voice for All Time: Essays on the Liturgy of the Catholic Church since the Second Vatican Council,* ed. C. Francis and M. Lynch (Bristol, 1994), 65–66.

fraught with difficulty, but the difficulties would be reduced if a *ritus communis* were to act (as is to some degree already happening) as the stable foundation for such liturgical development.

Secondly, the postconciliar rite could serve as the fundamental liturgical instrument for groups of Catholic-minded separated Western Christians, in practice, Anglicans and Lutherans, who wish to enter Catholic unity in some corporate way. It is not always realized that such Anglicans and Lutherans do not necessarily come from parts of those bodies accustomed to a high ritual form of worship. Some Anglicans attracted to Rome at the present juncture of world Christendom are Evangelicals by background; some Lutherans in a similar position are strangers to the liturgical high church Lutheranism associated with the Lund Movement in the Church of Sweden.

Finally, of course, the *ritus communis* would continue to be used in those parishes and religious communities of the Latin church that do not wish to recover the historical and spiritual patrimony of the Latin rite in a fuller form. The mistake to which poor advice led Paul VI of depriving many of the faithful of a hitherto canonical, indeed mandatory, rite to which they were attached must not be made again.

I have said little about liturgical offices other than the Eucharist: this is because the Mass is in a

"blessed fruits of the reform"
Paul VI

class of its own. It is the sun around which the celebration of the other sacraments revolves, and to which the stardust of the nonsacramental rites, from Vespers to the Blessing of an Abbess, composes clouds of witnesses. If the celebration of the Mass is adjusted to meet the criticism of contemporary use and abuse mounted in the historical, sociological-anthropological, and cultural-artistic sections of this study, then much that is valuable in the work of the liturgical reformers on the other offices (continuing, after all, the rubrical revision of Breviary, Pontifical, and Ritual from 1948 onward) will fall into place.

ENVOI

Hans Urs von Balthasar wrote:

> No liturgy designed by men could be "worthy" of
> the subject of their homage, of God at whose throne
> the heavenly choirs prostrate themselves with cov-
> ered faces, having cast off their crowns and orna-
> ments before offering adoration. The attempt to
> return to him who "created all according to his
> will" the honour that all creatures received must
> *a priori* compel to its knees an earthly community
> of sinners. *Domine, non sum dignus!* If such a com-
> munity, meeting for praise and worship, should
> have anything else in mind than adoration and
> self-oblation—for example, self-development or any
> other project in which they place themselves the-
> matically in context next to the Lord who is to
> be worshipped—then they naïvely deceive them-
> selves. This topic can be touched only with fear
> and trembling.[1]

That is the spirit in which I have tried to make
this plea; it is also a warning of the inevitable

[1] H. U. von Balthasar, "The Grandeur of the Liturgy",
Communio 5, no. 4 (1978), 344.

limitations of both reform and "restoration" in this area and an invitation to continue the discussion "for the praise and glory of his Name" — and if so then truly "for our good and that of all his (holy) Church".

INDEX

actuosa participatio, 65–69
Ainslie, John, 108
Andrieu, Msgr. Michel, 38
antidevotionalism, 23–26
archaism, 100
Archer, Anthony, 63
architecture, 88–91
Austin, J. L., 114

Barth, Karl, 20
Baumstark, Anton, 59–60
Bea, Augustin, 46
Beauduin, Dom Lambert, 12
Blau, Felix Anton, 26
Botte, Dom Bernard, 12–14,
    16, 38, 45–46
Bradshaw, Paul, 60
Bugnini, Annibale, 78

Casel, Dom Odo, 16, 45
celebrant, role at Mass,
    64–65
chant, 103–6
Christ, as High Priest, 68
community, 33, 40–41, 62,
    69, 79; development of,
    42–43
comparative liturgy, 59–60
Comte, Auguste, 98

Conlon, Anthony, 67–68
Crichton, Msgr. J. D., 67

d'Asnières, Abbé Jubé, 29
Dalmais, Irénée-Henri, 58
Day, Thomas, 108
de Lubac, Henri, 97–99
Demant, Vigo, 87–88
didacticism, 25, 32
Dilthey, Wilhelm, 57
Divini Cultus, (Pope Pius XI),
    105
Douglas, Mary, 71–76
Dura-Europos, 91–92

Elliott, Msgr. Peter, 118
Enlightenment, 17–18, 81,
    96; moderate, 17, 30–35;
    radical, 21–24, 26–29

Flanagan, Kieran, 54–66,
    69–71, 81–82
flow, 79–81
Franklin, R. W., 41–42

Guardini, Romano, 29
Guéranger, Dom Prosper,
    13, 40–43, 55, 103–4